NOTARY INFORMATION

Name:

Address:

Phone Number: **Fax Number:**

Email Address:

LOG BOOK INFORMATION

Log Book Number:

Start Date: **End Date:**

NOTARY RECORD

Printed Name and Address of Signer:

Phone Number:

Email:

Signer's Signature:

Thumb Print:

Service Performed:
- ○ Oath
- ○ Acknowledgment
- ○ Jurat
- ○ Other:

Identification:
- ○ I.D. Card
- ○ Drivers License
- ○ Passport
- ○ Other:
- ○ Credible Witness
- ○ Known Personally

I.D. Number:

Issued By:

Issued Date:

Expiration Date:

Document Type:

Date/Time Notarized: AM PM

Document Date:

Fee Charged:

Printed Name and Address of Witness:

Phone Number:

Email:

Witness' Signature:

Comments:

Record Number:
1

NOTARY RECORD

Printed Name and Address of Signer:

Phone Number:

Email:

Signer's Signature:

Thumb Print:

Service Performed:
- ○ Oath
- ○ Acknowledgment
- ○ Jurat
- ○ Other:

Identification:
- ○ I.D. Card
- ○ Drivers License
- ○ Passport
- ○ Other:
- ○ Credible Witness
- ○ Known Personally

I.D. Number:

Issued By:

Issued Date:

Expiration Date:

Document Type:

Date/Time Notarized: AM PM

Document Date:

Fee Charged:

Printed Name and Address of Witness:

Phone Number:

Email:

Witness' Signature:

Comments:

Record Number:
2

NOTARY RECORD

Printed Name and Address of Signer:	Phone Number:	Thumb Print:
	Email:	
	Signer's Signature:	

Service Performed:	Identification:	I.D. Number:	
○ Oath	○ I.D. Card ○ Credible Witness		
○ Acknowledgment	○ Drivers License ○ Known Personally	Issued By:	
○ Jurat	○ Passport	Issued Date:	Expiration Date:
○ Other:	○ Other:		
Document Type:	Date/Time Notarized: AM PM	Document Date:	Fee Charged:

Printed Name and Address of Witness:	Phone Number:
	Email:
	Witness' Signature:

Comments:	Record Number: **3**

NOTARY RECORD

Printed Name and Address of Signer:	Phone Number:	Thumb Print:
	Email:	
	Signer's Signature:	

Service Performed:	Identification:	I.D. Number:	
○ Oath	○ I.D. Card ○ Credible Witness		
○ Acknowledgment	○ Drivers License ○ Known Personally	Issued By:	
○ Jurat	○ Passport	Issued Date:	Expiration Date:
○ Other:	○ Other:		
Document Type:	Date/Time Notarized: AM PM	Document Date:	Fee Charged:

Printed Name and Address of Witness:	Phone Number:
	Email:
	Witness' Signature:

Comments:	Record Number: **4**

NOTARY RECORD

Printed Name and Address of Signer:

Phone Number:

Email:

Signer's Signature:

Thumb Print:

Service Performed:
- ○ Oath
- ○ Acknowledgment
- ○ Jurat
- ○ Other:

Identification:
- ○ I.D. Card
- ○ Drivers License
- ○ Passport
- ○ Other:
- ○ Credible Witness
- ○ Known Personally

I.D. Number:

Issued By:

Issued Date: | **Expiration Date:**

Document Type: | **Date/Time Notarized:** AM PM | **Document Date:** | **Fee Charged:**

Printed Name and Address of Witness:

Phone Number:

Email:

Witness' Signature:

Comments:

Record Number: 5

NOTARY RECORD

Printed Name and Address of Signer:

Phone Number:

Email:

Signer's Signature:

Thumb Print:

Service Performed:
- ○ Oath
- ○ Acknowledgment
- ○ Jurat
- ○ Other:

Identification:
- ○ I.D. Card
- ○ Drivers License
- ○ Passport
- ○ Other:
- ○ Credible Witness
- ○ Known Personally

I.D. Number:

Issued By:

Issued Date: | **Expiration Date:**

Document Type: | **Date/Time Notarized:** AM PM | **Document Date:** | **Fee Charged:**

Printed Name and Address of Witness:

Phone Number:

Email:

Witness' Signature:

Comments:

Record Number: 6

NOTARY RECORD

Printed Name and Address of Signer:	**Phone Number:**	**Thumb Print:**
	Email:	
	Signer's Signature:	

Service Performed:	**Identification:**	**I.D. Number:**
O Oath	O I.D. Card O Credible Witness	
O Acknowledgment	O Drivers License O Known Personally	**Issued By:**
O Jurat	O Passport	
O Other:	O Other:	**Issued Date:** **Expiration Date:**

Document Type:	**Date/Time Notarized:** AM PM	**Document Date:**	**Fee Charged:**

Printed Name and Address of Witness:	**Phone Number:**
	Email:
	Witness' Signature:

Comments:	**Record Number:** **7**

NOTARY RECORD

Printed Name and Address of Signer:	**Phone Number:**	**Thumb Print:**
	Email:	
	Signer's Signature:	

Service Performed:	**Identification:**	**I.D. Number:**
O Oath	O I.D. Card O Credible Witness	
O Acknowledgment	O Drivers License O Known Personally	**Issued By:**
O Jurat	O Passport	
O Other:	O Other:	**Issued Date:** **Expiration Date:**

Document Type:	**Date/Time Notarized:** AM PM	**Document Date:**	**Fee Charged:**

Printed Name and Address of Witness:	**Phone Number:**
	Email:
	Witness' Signature:

Comments:	**Record Number:** **8**

NOTARY RECORD

Printed Name and Address of Signer:	Phone Number:	Thumb Print:
	Email:	
	Signer's Signature:	

Service Performed:	Identification:	I.D. Number:	
○ Oath	○ I.D. Card ○ Credible Witness		
○ Acknowledgment	○ Drivers License ○ Known Personally	Issued By:	
○ Jurat	○ Passport	Issued Date:	Expiration Date:
○ Other:	○ Other:		
Document Type:	**Date/Time Notarized:** AM PM	**Document Date:**	**Fee Charged:**

Printed Name and Address of Witness:	Phone Number:
	Email:
	Witness' Signature:

Comments:	Record Number: **9**

NOTARY RECORD

Printed Name and Address of Signer:	Phone Number:	Thumb Print:
	Email:	
	Signer's Signature:	

Service Performed:	Identification:	I.D. Number:	
○ Oath	○ I.D. Card ○ Credible Witness		
○ Acknowledgment	○ Drivers License ○ Known Personally	Issued By:	
○ Jurat	○ Passport	Issued Date:	Expiration Date:
○ Other:	○ Other:		
Document Type:	**Date/Time Notarized:** AM PM	**Document Date:**	**Fee Charged:**

Printed Name and Address of Witness:	Phone Number:
	Email:
	Witness' Signature:

Comments:	Record Number: **10**

NOTARY RECORD

Printed Name and Address of Signer:

Phone Number:

Email:

Signer's Signature:

Thumb Print:

Service Performed:
- O Oath
- O Acknowledgment
- O Jurat
- O Other:

Identification:
- O I.D. Card   O Credible Witness
- O Drivers License   O Known Personally
- O Passport
- O Other:

I.D. Number:

Issued By:

Issued Date:

Expiration Date:

Document Type:

Date/Time Notarized: AM / PM

Document Date:

Fee Charged:

Printed Name and Address of Witness:

Phone Number:

Email:

Witness' Signature:

Comments:

Record Number: 11

NOTARY RECORD

Printed Name and Address of Signer:

Phone Number:

Email:

Signer's Signature:

Thumb Print:

Service Performed:
- O Oath
- O Acknowledgment
- O Jurat
- O Other:

Identification:
- O I.D. Card   O Credible Witness
- O Drivers License   O Known Personally
- O Passport
- O Other:

I.D. Number:

Issued By:

Issued Date:

Expiration Date:

Document Type:

Date/Time Notarized: AM / PM

Document Date:

Fee Charged:

Printed Name and Address of Witness:

Phone Number:

Email:

Witness' Signature:

Comments:

Record Number: 12

NOTARY RECORD

Printed Name and Address of Signer:	Phone Number:	Thumb Print:
	Email:	
	Signer's Signature:	

Service Performed:
○ Oath
○ Acknowledgment
○ Jurat
○ Other:

Identification:
○ I.D. Card   ○ Credible Witness
○ Drivers License   ○ Known Personally
○ Passport
○ Other:

I.D. Number:

Issued By:

Issued Date: **Expiration Date:**

Document Type: **Date/Time Notarized:** AM PM   **Document Date:**   **Fee Charged:**

Printed Name and Address of Witness:	Phone Number:
	Email:
	Witness' Signature:

Comments: **Record Number:** 13

NOTARY RECORD

Printed Name and Address of Signer:	Phone Number:	Thumb Print:
	Email:	
	Signer's Signature:	

Service Performed:
○ Oath
○ Acknowledgment
○ Jurat
○ Other:

Identification:
○ I.D. Card   ○ Credible Witness
○ Drivers License   ○ Known Personally
○ Passport
○ Other:

I.D. Number:

Issued By:

Issued Date: **Expiration Date:**

Document Type: **Date/Time Notarized:** AM PM   **Document Date:**   **Fee Charged:**

Printed Name and Address of Witness:	Phone Number:
	Email:
	Witness' Signature:

Comments: **Record Number:** 14

NOTARY RECORD

Printed Name and Address of Signer:	Phone Number:	Thumb Print:
	Email:	
	Signer's Signature:	

Service Performed:	Identification:	I.D. Number:	
○ Oath	○ I.D. Card ○ Credible Witness		
○ Acknowledgment	○ Drivers License ○ Known Personally	Issued By:	
○ Jurat	○ Passport		
○ Other:	○ Other:	Issued Date:	Expiration Date:
Document Type:	Date/Time Notarized: AM PM	Document Date:	Fee Charged:

Printed Name and Address of Witness:	Phone Number:
	Email:
	Witness' Signature:

Comments:	Record Number: **15**

NOTARY RECORD

Printed Name and Address of Signer:	Phone Number:	Thumb Print:
	Email:	
	Signer's Signature:	

Service Performed:	Identification:	I.D. Number:	
○ Oath	○ I.D. Card ○ Credible Witness		
○ Acknowledgment	○ Drivers License ○ Known Personally	Issued By:	
○ Jurat	○ Passport		
○ Other:	○ Other:	Issued Date:	Expiration Date:
Document Type:	Date/Time Notarized: AM PM	Document Date:	Fee Charged:

Printed Name and Address of Witness:	Phone Number:
	Email:
	Witness' Signature:

Comments:	Record Number: **16**

NOTARY RECORD

Printed Name and Address of Signer:

Phone Number:

Email:

Signer's Signature:

Thumb Print:

Service Performed:
- ○ Oath
- ○ Acknowledgment
- ○ Jurat
- ○ Other:

Identification:
- ○ I.D. Card   ○ Credible Witness
- ○ Drivers License   ○ Known Personally
- ○ Passport
- ○ Other:

I.D. Number:

Issued By:

Issued Date:

Expiration Date:

Document Type:

Date/Time Notarized: AM / PM

Document Date:

Fee Charged:

Printed Name and Address of Witness:

Phone Number:

Email:

Witness' Signature:

Comments:

Record Number:
17

NOTARY RECORD

Printed Name and Address of Signer:

Phone Number:

Email:

Signer's Signature:

Thumb Print:

Service Performed:
- ○ Oath
- ○ Acknowledgment
- ○ Jurat
- ○ Other:

Identification:
- ○ I.D. Card   ○ Credible Witness
- ○ Drivers License   ○ Known Personally
- ○ Passport
- ○ Other:

I.D. Number:

Issued By:

Issued Date:

Expiration Date:

Document Type:

Date/Time Notarized: AM / PM

Document Date:

Fee Charged:

Printed Name and Address of Witness:

Phone Number:

Email:

Witness' Signature:

Comments:

Record Number:
18

NOTARY RECORD

Printed Name and Address of Signer:	Phone Number:	Thumb Print:
	Email:	
	Signer's Signature:	

Service Performed:	Identification:		I.D. Number:	
O Oath	O I.D. Card	O Credible Witness		
O Acknowledgment	O Drivers License	O Known Personally	Issued By:	
O Jurat	O Passport		Issued Date:	Expiration Date:
O Other:	O Other:			
Document Type:	Date/Time Notarized:	AM PM	Document Date:	Fee Charged:

Printed Name and Address of Witness:	Phone Number:
	Email:
	Witness' Signature:

Comments:	Record Number: **19**

NOTARY RECORD

Printed Name and Address of Signer:	Phone Number:	Thumb Print:
	Email:	
	Signer's Signature:	

Service Performed:	Identification:		I.D. Number:	
O Oath	O I.D. Card	O Credible Witness		
O Acknowledgment	O Drivers License	O Known Personally	Issued By:	
O Jurat	O Passport		Issued Date:	Expiration Date:
O Other:	O Other:			
Document Type:	Date/Time Notarized:	AM PM	Document Date:	Fee Charged:

Printed Name and Address of Witness:	Phone Number:
	Email:
	Witness' Signature:

Comments:	Record Number: **20**

NOTARY RECORD

Printed Name and Address of Signer:

Phone Number:

Email:

Signer's Signature:

Thumb Print:

Service Performed:
- ○ Oath
- ○ Acknowledgment
- ○ Jurat
- ○ Other:

Identification:
- ○ I.D. Card
- ○ Drivers License
- ○ Passport
- ○ Other:
- ○ Credible Witness
- ○ Known Personally

I.D. Number:

Issued By:

Issued Date:

Expiration Date:

Document Type:

Date/Time Notarized: AM PM

Document Date:

Fee Charged:

Printed Name and Address of Witness:

Phone Number:

Email:

Witness' Signature:

Comments:

Record Number: 21

NOTARY RECORD

Printed Name and Address of Signer:

Phone Number:

Email:

Signer's Signature:

Thumb Print:

Service Performed:
- ○ Oath
- ○ Acknowledgment
- ○ Jurat
- ○ Other:

Identification:
- ○ I.D. Card
- ○ Drivers License
- ○ Passport
- ○ Other:
- ○ Credible Witness
- ○ Known Personally

I.D. Number:

Issued By:

Issued Date:

Expiration Date:

Document Type:

Date/Time Notarized: AM PM

Document Date:

Fee Charged:

Printed Name and Address of Witness:

Phone Number:

Email:

Witness' Signature:

Comments:

Record Number: 22

NOTARY RECORD

Printed Name and Address of Signer:	Phone Number:	Thumb Print:
	Email:	
	Signer's Signature:	

Service Performed:	Identification:	I.D. Number:	
O Oath	O I.D. Card O Credible Witness		
O Acknowledgment	O Drivers License O Known Personally	Issued By:	
O Jurat	O Passport		
O Other:	O Other:	Issued Date:	Expiration Date:
Document Type:	Date/Time Notarized: AM PM	Document Date:	Fee Charged:

Printed Name and Address of Witness:	Phone Number:
	Email:
	Witness' Signature:

Comments:	Record Number: **23**

NOTARY RECORD

Printed Name and Address of Signer:	Phone Number:	Thumb Print:
	Email:	
	Signer's Signature:	

Service Performed:	Identification:	I.D. Number:	
O Oath	O I.D. Card O Credible Witness		
O Acknowledgment	O Drivers License O Known Personally	Issued By:	
O Jurat	O Passport		
O Other:	O Other:	Issued Date:	Expiration Date:
Document Type:	Date/Time Notarized: AM PM	Document Date:	Fee Charged:

Printed Name and Address of Witness:	Phone Number:
	Email:
	Witness' Signature:

Comments:	Record Number: **24**

NOTARY RECORD

Printed Name and Address of Signer:	Phone Number:	Thumb Print:
	Email:	
	Signer's Signature:	

Service Performed:	Identification:	I.D. Number:	
○ Oath	○ I.D. Card ○ Credible Witness		
○ Acknowledgment	○ Drivers License ○ Known Personally	Issued By:	
○ Jurat	○ Passport		
○ Other:	○ Other:	Issued Date:	Expiration Date:
Document Type:	Date/Time Notarized: AM PM	Document Date:	Fee Charged:

Printed Name and Address of Witness:	Phone Number:
	Email:
	Witness' Signature:

Comments:	Record Number: **25**

NOTARY RECORD

Printed Name and Address of Signer:	Phone Number:	Thumb Print:
	Email:	
	Signer's Signature:	

Service Performed:	Identification:	I.D. Number:	
○ Oath	○ I.D. Card ○ Credible Witness		
○ Acknowledgment	○ Drivers License ○ Known Personally	Issued By:	
○ Jurat	○ Passport		
○ Other:	○ Other:	Issued Date:	Expiration Date:
Document Type:	Date/Time Notarized: AM PM	Document Date:	Fee Charged:

Printed Name and Address of Witness:	Phone Number:
	Email:
	Witness' Signature:

Comments:	Record Number: **26**

NOTARY RECORD

Printed Name and Address of Signer:	Phone Number:	Thumb Print:
	Email:	
	Signer's Signature:	

Service Performed:	Identification:	I.D. Number:	
○ Oath	○ I.D. Card ○ Credible Witness		
○ Acknowledgment	○ Drivers License ○ Known Personally	Issued By:	
○ Jurat	○ Passport		
○ Other:	○ Other:	Issued Date:	Expiration Date:
Document Type:	Date/Time Notarized: AM PM	Document Date:	Fee Charged:

Printed Name and Address of Witness:	Phone Number:
	Email:
	Witness' Signature:

Comments:	Record Number: **27**

NOTARY RECORD

Printed Name and Address of Signer:	Phone Number:	Thumb Print:
	Email:	
	Signer's Signature:	

Service Performed:	Identification:	I.D. Number:	
○ Oath	○ I.D. Card ○ Credible Witness		
○ Acknowledgment	○ Drivers License ○ Known Personally	Issued By:	
○ Jurat	○ Passport		
○ Other:	○ Other:	Issued Date:	Expiration Date:
Document Type:	Date/Time Notarized: AM PM	Document Date:	Fee Charged:

Printed Name and Address of Witness:	Phone Number:
	Email:
	Witness' Signature:

Comments:	Record Number: **28**

NOTARY RECORD

Printed Name and Address of Signer:

Phone Number:

Email:

Signer's Signature:

Thumb Print:

Service Performed:
- O Oath
- O Acknowledgment
- O Jurat
- O Other:

Identification:
- O I.D. Card
- O Drivers License
- O Passport
- O Other:
- O Credible Witness
- O Known Personally

I.D. Number:

Issued By:

Issued Date:

Expiration Date:

Document Type:

Date/Time Notarized: AM PM

Document Date:

Fee Charged:

Printed Name and Address of Witness:

Phone Number:

Email:

Witness' Signature:

Comments:

Record Number:
29

NOTARY RECORD

Printed Name and Address of Signer:

Phone Number:

Email:

Signer's Signature:

Thumb Print:

Service Performed:
- O Oath
- O Acknowledgment
- O Jurat
- O Other:

Identification:
- O I.D. Card
- O Drivers License
- O Passport
- O Other:
- O Credible Witness
- O Known Personally

I.D. Number:

Issued By:

Issued Date:

Expiration Date:

Document Type:

Date/Time Notarized: AM PM

Document Date:

Fee Charged:

Printed Name and Address of Witness:

Phone Number:

Email:

Witness' Signature:

Comments:

Record Number:
30

NOTARY RECORD

Printed Name and Address of Signer:	Phone Number:	Thumb Print:
	Email:	
	Signer's Signature:	

Service Performed:
- ○ Oath
- ○ Acknowledgment
- ○ Jurat
- ○ Other:

Identification:
- ○ I.D. Card   ○ Credible Witness
- ○ Drivers License ○ Known Personally
- ○ Passport
- ○ Other:

I.D. Number:	
Issued By:	
Issued Date:	Expiration Date:

Document Type:	Date/Time Notarized: AM / PM	Document Date:	Fee Charged:

Printed Name and Address of Witness:	Phone Number:
	Email:
	Witness' Signature:

Comments:

Record Number: 31

NOTARY RECORD

Printed Name and Address of Signer:	Phone Number:	Thumb Print:
	Email:	
	Signer's Signature:	

Service Performed:
- ○ Oath
- ○ Acknowledgment
- ○ Jurat
- ○ Other:

Identification:
- ○ I.D. Card   ○ Credible Witness
- ○ Drivers License ○ Known Personally
- ○ Passport
- ○ Other:

I.D. Number:	
Issued By:	
Issued Date:	Expiration Date:

Document Type:	Date/Time Notarized: AM / PM	Document Date:	Fee Charged:

Printed Name and Address of Witness:	Phone Number:
	Email:
	Witness' Signature:

Comments:

Record Number: 32

NOTARY RECORD

Printed Name and Address of Signer:

Phone Number:

Email:

Signer's Signature:

Thumb Print:

Service Performed:
- ○ Oath
- ○ Acknowledgment
- ○ Jurat
- ○ Other:

Identification:
- ○ I.D. Card
- ○ Drivers License
- ○ Passport
- ○ Other:
- ○ Credible Witness
- ○ Known Personally

I.D. Number:

Issued By:

Issued Date:

Expiration Date:

Document Type:

Date/Time Notarized: AM PM

Document Date:

Fee Charged:

Printed Name and Address of Witness:

Phone Number:

Email:

Witness' Signature:

Comments:

Record Number:
33

NOTARY RECORD

Printed Name and Address of Signer:

Phone Number:

Email:

Signer's Signature:

Thumb Print:

Service Performed:
- ○ Oath
- ○ Acknowledgment
- ○ Jurat
- ○ Other:

Identification:
- ○ I.D. Card
- ○ Drivers License
- ○ Passport
- ○ Other:
- ○ Credible Witness
- ○ Known Personally

I.D. Number:

Issued By:

Issued Date:

Expiration Date:

Document Type:

Date/Time Notarized: AM PM

Document Date:

Fee Charged:

Printed Name and Address of Witness:

Phone Number:

Email:

Witness' Signature:

Comments:

Record Number:
34

NOTARY RECORD

Printed Name and Address of Signer:

Phone Number:

Email:

Signer's Signature:

Thumb Print:

Service Performed:
- ○ Oath
- ○ Acknowledgment
- ○ Jurat
- ○ Other:

Identification:
- ○ I.D. Card ○ Credible Witness
- ○ Drivers License ○ Known Personally
- ○ Passport
- ○ Other:

I.D. Number:

Issued By:

Issued Date:

Expiration Date:

Document Type:

Date/Time Notarized: AM PM

Document Date:

Fee Charged:

Printed Name and Address of Witness:

Phone Number:

Email:

Witness' Signature:

Comments:

Record Number: 35

NOTARY RECORD

Printed Name and Address of Signer:

Phone Number:

Email:

Signer's Signature:

Thumb Print:

Service Performed:
- ○ Oath
- ○ Acknowledgment
- ○ Jurat
- ○ Other:

Identification:
- ○ I.D. Card ○ Credible Witness
- ○ Drivers License ○ Known Personally
- ○ Passport
- ○ Other:

I.D. Number:

Issued By:

Issued Date:

Expiration Date:

Document Type:

Date/Time Notarized: AM PM

Document Date:

Fee Charged:

Printed Name and Address of Witness:

Phone Number:

Email:

Witness' Signature:

Comments:

Record Number: 36

NOTARY RECORD

Printed Name and Address of Signer:	Phone Number:	Thumb Print:
	Email:	
	Signer's Signature:	

Service Performed:	Identification:		I.D. Number:	
○ Oath	○ I.D. Card	○ Credible Witness		
○ Acknowledgment	○ Drivers License	○ Known Personally	Issued By:	
○ Jurat	○ Passport		Issued Date:	Expiration Date:
○ Other:	○ Other:			
Document Type:	Date/Time Notarized:	AM PM	Document Date:	Fee Charged:

Printed Name and Address of Witness:	Phone Number:
	Email:
	Witness' Signature:

Comments:	Record Number: **37**

NOTARY RECORD

Printed Name and Address of Signer:	Phone Number:	Thumb Print:
	Email:	
	Signer's Signature:	

Service Performed:	Identification:		I.D. Number:	
○ Oath	○ I.D. Card	○ Credible Witness		
○ Acknowledgment	○ Drivers License	○ Known Personally	Issued By:	
○ Jurat	○ Passport		Issued Date:	Expiration Date:
○ Other:	○ Other:			
Document Type:	Date/Time Notarized:	AM PM	Document Date:	Fee Charged:

Printed Name and Address of Witness:	Phone Number:
	Email:
	Witness' Signature:

Comments:	Record Number: **38**

NOTARY RECORD

Printed Name and Address of Signer:	Phone Number:	Thumb Print:
	Email:	
	Signer's Signature:	

Service Performed:	Identification:	I.D. Number:
○ Oath	○ I.D. Card ○ Credible Witness	
○ Acknowledgment	○ Drivers License ○ Known Personally	Issued By:
○ Jurat	○ Passport	Issued Date: / Expiration Date:
○ Other:	○ Other:	
Document Type:	Date/Time Notarized: AM / PM	Document Date: / Fee Charged:

Printed Name and Address of Witness:	Phone Number:
	Email:
	Witness' Signature:

Comments:

Record Number: 39

NOTARY RECORD

Printed Name and Address of Signer:	Phone Number:	Thumb Print:
	Email:	
	Signer's Signature:	

Service Performed:	Identification:	I.D. Number:
○ Oath	○ I.D. Card ○ Credible Witness	
○ Acknowledgment	○ Drivers License ○ Known Personally	Issued By:
○ Jurat	○ Passport	Issued Date: / Expiration Date:
○ Other:	○ Other:	
Document Type:	Date/Time Notarized: AM / PM	Document Date: / Fee Charged:

Printed Name and Address of Witness:	Phone Number:
	Email:
	Witness' Signature:

Comments:

Record Number: 40

NOTARY RECORD

Printed Name and Address of Signer:	Phone Number:	Thumb Print:
	Email:	
	Signer's Signature:	

Service Performed:	Identification:	I.D. Number:
O Oath	O I.D. Card O Credible Witness	
O Acknowledgment	O Drivers License O Known Personally	Issued By:
O Jurat	O Passport	
O Other:	O Other:	Issued Date: Expiration Date:

Document Type:	Date/Time Notarized: AM PM	Document Date:	Fee Charged:

Printed Name and Address of Witness:	Phone Number:
	Email:
	Witness' Signature:

Comments:	Record Number: **41**

NOTARY RECORD

Printed Name and Address of Signer:	Phone Number:	Thumb Print:
	Email:	
	Signer's Signature:	

Service Performed:	Identification:	I.D. Number:
O Oath	O I.D. Card O Credible Witness	
O Acknowledgment	O Drivers License O Known Personally	Issued By:
O Jurat	O Passport	
O Other:	O Other:	Issued Date: Expiration Date:

Document Type:	Date/Time Notarized: AM PM	Document Date:	Fee Charged:

Printed Name and Address of Witness:	Phone Number:
	Email:
	Witness' Signature:

Comments:	Record Number: **42**

NOTARY RECORD

Printed Name and Address of Signer:

Phone Number:

Email:

Signer's Signature:

Thumb Print:

Service Performed:
- ○ Oath
- ○ Acknowledgment
- ○ Jurat
- ○ Other:

Identification:
- ○ I.D. Card   ○ Credible Witness
- ○ Drivers License   ○ Known Personally
- ○ Passport
- ○ Other:

I.D. Number:

Issued By:

Issued Date: **Expiration Date:**

Document Type:

Date/Time Notarized: AM / PM

Document Date: **Fee Charged:**

Printed Name and Address of Witness:

Phone Number:

Email:

Witness' Signature:

Comments:

Record Number: 43

NOTARY RECORD

Printed Name and Address of Signer:

Phone Number:

Email:

Signer's Signature:

Thumb Print:

Service Performed:
- ○ Oath
- ○ Acknowledgment
- ○ Jurat
- ○ Other:

Identification:
- ○ I.D. Card   ○ Credible Witness
- ○ Drivers License   ○ Known Personally
- ○ Passport
- ○ Other:

I.D. Number:

Issued By:

Issued Date: **Expiration Date:**

Document Type:

Date/Time Notarized: AM / PM

Document Date: **Fee Charged:**

Printed Name and Address of Witness:

Phone Number:

Email:

Witness' Signature:

Comments:

Record Number: 44

NOTARY RECORD

Printed Name and Address of Signer:

Phone Number:

Email:

Signer's Signature:

Thumb Print:

Service Performed:
- ○ Oath
- ○ Acknowledgment
- ○ Jurat
- ○ Other:

Identification:
- ○ I.D. Card
- ○ Drivers License
- ○ Passport
- ○ Other:
- ○ Credible Witness
- ○ Known Personally

I.D. Number:

Issued By:

Issued Date: **Expiration Date:**

Document Type:

Date/Time Notarized: AM PM

Document Date:

Fee Charged:

Printed Name and Address of Witness:

Phone Number:

Email:

Witness' Signature:

Comments:

Record Number:
45

NOTARY RECORD

Printed Name and Address of Signer:

Phone Number:

Email:

Signer's Signature:

Thumb Print:

Service Performed:
- ○ Oath
- ○ Acknowledgment
- ○ Jurat
- ○ Other:

Identification:
- ○ I.D. Card
- ○ Drivers License
- ○ Passport
- ○ Other:
- ○ Credible Witness
- ○ Known Personally

I.D. Number:

Issued By:

Issued Date: **Expiration Date:**

Document Type:

Date/Time Notarized: AM PM

Document Date:

Fee Charged:

Printed Name and Address of Witness:

Phone Number:

Email:

Witness' Signature:

Comments:

Record Number:
46

NOTARY RECORD

Printed Name and Address of Signer:

Phone Number:

Email:

Signer's Signature:

Thumb Print:

Service Performed:
- ○ Oath
- ○ Acknowledgment
- ○ Jurat
- ○ Other:

Identification:
- ○ I.D. Card   ○ Credible Witness
- ○ Drivers License   ○ Known Personally
- ○ Passport
- ○ Other:

I.D. Number:

Issued By:

Issued Date: | **Expiration Date:**

Document Type:

Date/Time Notarized: AM PM

Document Date: | **Fee Charged:**

Printed Name and Address of Witness:

Phone Number:

Email:

Witness' Signature:

Comments:

Record Number:
47

NOTARY RECORD

Printed Name and Address of Signer:

Phone Number:

Email:

Signer's Signature:

Thumb Print:

Service Performed:
- ○ Oath
- ○ Acknowledgment
- ○ Jurat
- ○ Other:

Identification:
- ○ I.D. Card   ○ Credible Witness
- ○ Drivers License   ○ Known Personally
- ○ Passport
- ○ Other:

I.D. Number:

Issued By:

Issued Date: | **Expiration Date:**

Document Type:

Date/Time Notarized: AM PM

Document Date: | **Fee Charged:**

Printed Name and Address of Witness:

Phone Number:

Email:

Witness' Signature:

Comments:

Record Number:
48

NOTARY RECORD

Printed Name and Address of Signer:

Phone Number:

Email:

Signer's Signature:

Thumb Print:

Service Performed:
- ○ Oath
- ○ Acknowledgment
- ○ Jurat
- ○ Other:

Identification:
- ○ I.D. Card
- ○ Drivers License
- ○ Passport
- ○ Other:
- ○ Credible Witness
- ○ Known Personally

I.D. Number:

Issued By:

Issued Date:

Expiration Date:

Document Type:

Date/Time Notarized: AM PM

Document Date:

Fee Charged:

Printed Name and Address of Witness:

Phone Number:

Email:

Witness' Signature:

Comments:

Record Number:
49

NOTARY RECORD

Printed Name and Address of Signer:

Phone Number:

Email:

Signer's Signature:

Thumb Print:

Service Performed:
- ○ Oath
- ○ Acknowledgment
- ○ Jurat
- ○ Other:

Identification:
- ○ I.D. Card
- ○ Drivers License
- ○ Passport
- ○ Other:
- ○ Credible Witness
- ○ Known Personally

I.D. Number:

Issued By:

Issued Date:

Expiration Date:

Document Type:

Date/Time Notarized: AM PM

Document Date:

Fee Charged:

Printed Name and Address of Witness:

Phone Number:

Email:

Witness' Signature:

Comments:

Record Number:
50

NOTARY RECORD

Printed Name and Address of Signer:	Phone Number:	Thumb Print:
	Email:	
	Signer's Signature:	

Service Performed:	Identification:	I.D. Number:
○ Oath	○ I.D. Card ○ Credible Witness	
○ Acknowledgment	○ Drivers License ○ Known Personally	Issued By:
○ Jurat	○ Passport	
○ Other:	○ Other:	Issued Date: Expiration Date:

Document Type:	Date/Time Notarized: AM / PM	Document Date:	Fee Charged:

Printed Name and Address of Witness:	Phone Number:
	Email:
	Witness' Signature:

Comments:	Record Number: **51**

NOTARY RECORD

Printed Name and Address of Signer:	Phone Number:	Thumb Print:
	Email:	
	Signer's Signature:	

Service Performed:	Identification:	I.D. Number:
○ Oath	○ I.D. Card ○ Credible Witness	
○ Acknowledgment	○ Drivers License ○ Known Personally	Issued By:
○ Jurat	○ Passport	
○ Other:	○ Other:	Issued Date: Expiration Date:

Document Type:	Date/Time Notarized: AM / PM	Document Date:	Fee Charged:

Printed Name and Address of Witness:	Phone Number:
	Email:
	Witness' Signature:

Comments:	Record Number: **52**

NOTARY RECORD

Printed Name and Address of Signer:

Phone Number:

Email:

Signer's Signature:

Thumb Print:

Service Performed:
- ○ Oath
- ○ Acknowledgment
- ○ Jurat
- ○ Other:

Identification:
- ○ I.D. Card
- ○ Drivers License
- ○ Passport
- ○ Other:
- ○ Credible Witness
- ○ Known Personally

I.D. Number:

Issued By:

Issued Date:

Expiration Date:

Document Type:

Date/Time Notarized: AM / PM

Document Date:

Fee Charged:

Printed Name and Address of Witness:

Phone Number:

Email:

Witness' Signature:

Comments:

Record Number:
53

NOTARY RECORD

Printed Name and Address of Signer:

Phone Number:

Email:

Signer's Signature:

Thumb Print:

Service Performed:
- ○ Oath
- ○ Acknowledgment
- ○ Jurat
- ○ Other:

Identification:
- ○ I.D. Card
- ○ Drivers License
- ○ Passport
- ○ Other:
- ○ Credible Witness
- ○ Known Personally

I.D. Number:

Issued By:

Issued Date:

Expiration Date:

Document Type:

Date/Time Notarized: AM / PM

Document Date:

Fee Charged:

Printed Name and Address of Witness:

Phone Number:

Email:

Witness' Signature:

Comments:

Record Number:
54

NOTARY RECORD

Printed Name and Address of Signer:	Phone Number:	Thumb Print:
	Email:	
	Signer's Signature:	

Service Performed:	Identification:	I.D. Number:
O Oath	O I.D. Card O Credible Witness	
O Acknowledgment	O Drivers License O Known Personally	Issued By:
O Jurat	O Passport	Issued Date: Expiration Date:
O Other:	O Other:	
Document Type:	Date/Time Notarized: AM PM	Document Date: Fee Charged:

Printed Name and Address of Witness:	Phone Number:
	Email:
	Witness' Signature:

Comments:	Record Number: **55**

NOTARY RECORD

Printed Name and Address of Signer:	Phone Number:	Thumb Print:
	Email:	
	Signer's Signature:	

Service Performed:	Identification:	I.D. Number:
O Oath	O I.D. Card O Credible Witness	
O Acknowledgment	O Drivers License O Known Personally	Issued By:
O Jurat	O Passport	Issued Date: Expiration Date:
O Other:	O Other:	
Document Type:	Date/Time Notarized: AM PM	Document Date: Fee Charged:

Printed Name and Address of Witness:	Phone Number:
	Email:
	Witness' Signature:

Comments:	Record Number: **56**

NOTARY RECORD

Printed Name and Address of Signer:

Phone Number:

Email:

Signer's Signature:

Thumb Print:

Service Performed:
- ○ Oath
- ○ Acknowledgment
- ○ Jurat
- ○ Other:

Identification:
- ○ I.D. Card
- ○ Drivers License
- ○ Passport
- ○ Other:
- ○ Credible Witness
- ○ Known Personally

I.D. Number:

Issued By:

Issued Date:

Expiration Date:

Document Type:

Date/Time Notarized: AM / PM

Document Date:

Fee Charged:

Printed Name and Address of Witness:

Phone Number:

Email:

Witness' Signature:

Comments:

Record Number: 57

NOTARY RECORD

Printed Name and Address of Signer:

Phone Number:

Email:

Signer's Signature:

Thumb Print:

Service Performed:
- ○ Oath
- ○ Acknowledgment
- ○ Jurat
- ○ Other:

Identification:
- ○ I.D. Card
- ○ Drivers License
- ○ Passport
- ○ Other:
- ○ Credible Witness
- ○ Known Personally

I.D. Number:

Issued By:

Issued Date:

Expiration Date:

Document Type:

Date/Time Notarized: AM / PM

Document Date:

Fee Charged:

Printed Name and Address of Witness:

Phone Number:

Email:

Witness' Signature:

Comments:

Record Number: 58

NOTARY RECORD

Printed Name and Address of Signer:	**Phone Number:**	**Thumb Print:**
	Email:	
	Signer's Signature:	

Service Performed:	**Identification:**	**I.D. Number:**	
○ Oath	○ I.D. Card ○ Credible Witness		
○ Acknowledgment	○ Drivers License ○ Known Personally	**Issued By:**	
○ Jurat	○ Passport		
○ Other:	○ Other:	**Issued Date:**	**Expiration Date:**
Document Type:	**Date/Time Notarized:** AM PM	**Document Date:**	**Fee Charged:**

Printed Name and Address of Witness:	**Phone Number:**	
	Email:	
	Witness' Signature:	

Comments:	**Record Number:**
	59

NOTARY RECORD

Printed Name and Address of Signer:	**Phone Number:**	**Thumb Print:**
	Email:	
	Signer's Signature:	

Service Performed:	**Identification:**	**I.D. Number:**	
○ Oath	○ I.D. Card ○ Credible Witness		
○ Acknowledgment	○ Drivers License ○ Known Personally	**Issued By:**	
○ Jurat	○ Passport		
○ Other:	○ Other:	**Issued Date:**	**Expiration Date:**
Document Type:	**Date/Time Notarized:** AM PM	**Document Date:**	**Fee Charged:**

Printed Name and Address of Witness:	**Phone Number:**	
	Email:	
	Witness' Signature:	

Comments:	**Record Number:**
	60

NOTARY RECORD

Printed Name and Address of Signer:	Phone Number:	Thumb Print:
	Email:	
	Signer's Signature:	

Service Performed:	Identification:		I.D. Number:	
O Oath	O I.D. Card	O Credible Witness		
O Acknowledgment	O Drivers License	O Known Personally	Issued By:	
O Jurat	O Passport		Issued Date:	Expiration Date:
O Other:	O Other:			
Document Type:	Date/Time Notarized:	AM PM	Document Date:	Fee Charged:

Printed Name and Address of Witness:	Phone Number:
	Email:
	Witness' Signature:

Comments:	Record Number: **61**

NOTARY RECORD

Printed Name and Address of Signer:	Phone Number:	Thumb Print:
	Email:	
	Signer's Signature:	

Service Performed:	Identification:		I.D. Number:	
O Oath	O I.D. Card	O Credible Witness		
O Acknowledgment	O Drivers License	O Known Personally	Issued By:	
O Jurat	O Passport		Issued Date:	Expiration Date:
O Other:	O Other:			
Document Type:	Date/Time Notarized:	AM PM	Document Date:	Fee Charged:

Printed Name and Address of Witness:	Phone Number:
	Email:
	Witness' Signature:

Comments:	Record Number: **62**

NOTARY RECORD

Printed Name and Address of Signer:	Phone Number:	Thumb Print:
	Email:	
	Signer's Signature:	

Service Performed:
- ○ Oath
- ○ Acknowledgment
- ○ Jurat
- ○ Other:

Identification:
- ○ I.D. Card   ○ Credible Witness
- ○ Drivers License   ○ Known Personally
- ○ Passport
- ○ Other:

I.D. Number:	
Issued By:	
Issued Date:	Expiration Date:

Document Type:	Date/Time Notarized: AM / PM	Document Date:	Fee Charged:

Printed Name and Address of Witness:	Phone Number:
	Email:
	Witness' Signature:

Comments:	Record Number: **63**

NOTARY RECORD

Printed Name and Address of Signer:	Phone Number:	Thumb Print:
	Email:	
	Signer's Signature:	

Service Performed:
- ○ Oath
- ○ Acknowledgment
- ○ Jurat
- ○ Other:

Identification:
- ○ I.D. Card   ○ Credible Witness
- ○ Drivers License   ○ Known Personally
- ○ Passport
- ○ Other:

I.D. Number:	
Issued By:	
Issued Date:	Expiration Date:

Document Type:	Date/Time Notarized: AM / PM	Document Date:	Fee Charged:

Printed Name and Address of Witness:	Phone Number:
	Email:
	Witness' Signature:

Comments:	Record Number: **64**

NOTARY RECORD

Printed Name and Address of Signer:

Phone Number:

Email:

Signer's Signature:

Thumb Print:

Service Performed:
- ○ Oath
- ○ Acknowledgment
- ○ Jurat
- ○ Other:

Identification:
- ○ I.D. Card
- ○ Drivers License
- ○ Passport
- ○ Other:
- ○ Credible Witness
- ○ Known Personally

I.D. Number:

Issued By:

Issued Date:

Expiration Date:

Document Type:

Date/Time Notarized: AM PM

Document Date:

Fee Charged:

Printed Name and Address of Witness:

Phone Number:

Email:

Witness' Signature:

Comments:

Record Number: **65**

NOTARY RECORD

Printed Name and Address of Signer:

Phone Number:

Email:

Signer's Signature:

Thumb Print:

Service Performed:
- ○ Oath
- ○ Acknowledgment
- ○ Jurat
- ○ Other:

Identification:
- ○ I.D. Card
- ○ Drivers License
- ○ Passport
- ○ Other:
- ○ Credible Witness
- ○ Known Personally

I.D. Number:

Issued By:

Issued Date:

Expiration Date:

Document Type:

Date/Time Notarized: AM PM

Document Date:

Fee Charged:

Printed Name and Address of Witness:

Phone Number:

Email:

Witness' Signature:

Comments:

Record Number: **66**

NOTARY RECORD

Printed Name and Address of Signer:	Phone Number:	Thumb Print:
	Email:	
	Signer's Signature:	

Service Performed:	Identification:	I.D. Number:	
O Oath	O I.D. Card O Credible Witness		
O Acknowledgment	O Drivers License O Known Personally	Issued By:	
O Jurat	O Passport		
O Other:	O Other:	Issued Date:	Expiration Date:
Document Type:	Date/Time Notarized: AM / PM	Document Date:	Fee Charged:

Printed Name and Address of Witness:	Phone Number:
	Email:
	Witness' Signature:

Comments:	Record Number:
	67

NOTARY RECORD

Printed Name and Address of Signer:	Phone Number:	Thumb Print:
	Email:	
	Signer's Signature:	

Service Performed:	Identification:	I.D. Number:	
O Oath	O I.D. Card O Credible Witness		
O Acknowledgment	O Drivers License O Known Personally	Issued By:	
O Jurat	O Passport		
O Other:	O Other:	Issued Date:	Expiration Date:
Document Type:	Date/Time Notarized: AM / PM	Document Date:	Fee Charged:

Printed Name and Address of Witness:	Phone Number:
	Email:
	Witness' Signature:

Comments:	Record Number:
	68

NOTARY RECORD

Printed Name and Address of Signer:

Phone Number:

Email:

Signer's Signature:

Thumb Print:

Service Performed:
- ○ Oath
- ○ Acknowledgment
- ○ Jurat
- ○ Other:

Identification:
- ○ I.D. Card
- ○ Drivers License
- ○ Passport
- ○ Other:
- ○ Credible Witness
- ○ Known Personally

I.D. Number:

Issued By:

Issued Date:

Expiration Date:

Document Type:

Date/Time Notarized: AM PM

Document Date:

Fee Charged:

Printed Name and Address of Witness:

Phone Number:

Email:

Witness' Signature:

Comments:

Record Number: 69

NOTARY RECORD

Printed Name and Address of Signer:

Phone Number:

Email:

Signer's Signature:

Thumb Print:

Service Performed:
- ○ Oath
- ○ Acknowledgment
- ○ Jurat
- ○ Other:

Identification:
- ○ I.D. Card
- ○ Drivers License
- ○ Passport
- ○ Other:
- ○ Credible Witness
- ○ Known Personally

I.D. Number:

Issued By:

Issued Date:

Expiration Date:

Document Type:

Date/Time Notarized: AM PM

Document Date:

Fee Charged:

Printed Name and Address of Witness:

Phone Number:

Email:

Witness' Signature:

Comments:

Record Number: 70

NOTARY RECORD

Printed Name and Address of Signer:	Phone Number:	Thumb Print:
	Email:	
	Signer's Signature:	

Service Performed:
- ○ Oath
- ○ Acknowledgment
- ○ Jurat
- ○ Other:

Identification:
- ○ I.D. Card   ○ Credible Witness
- ○ Drivers License   ○ Known Personally
- ○ Passport
- ○ Other:

I.D. Number:	
Issued By:	
Issued Date:	Expiration Date:

Document Type:	Date/Time Notarized: AM PM	Document Date:	Fee Charged:

Printed Name and Address of Witness:	Phone Number:
	Email:
	Witness' Signature:

Comments:

Record Number: 71

NOTARY RECORD

Printed Name and Address of Signer:	Phone Number:	Thumb Print:
	Email:	
	Signer's Signature:	

Service Performed:
- ○ Oath
- ○ Acknowledgment
- ○ Jurat
- ○ Other:

Identification:
- ○ I.D. Card   ○ Credible Witness
- ○ Drivers License   ○ Known Personally
- ○ Passport
- ○ Other:

I.D. Number:	
Issued By:	
Issued Date:	Expiration Date:

Document Type:	Date/Time Notarized: AM PM	Document Date:	Fee Charged:

Printed Name and Address of Witness:	Phone Number:
	Email:
	Witness' Signature:

Comments:

Record Number: 72

NOTARY RECORD

Printed Name and Address of Signer:	Phone Number:	Thumb Print:
	Email:	
	Signer's Signature:	

Service Performed:	Identification:	I.D. Number:
○ Oath	○ I.D. Card ○ Credible Witness	
○ Acknowledgment	○ Drivers License ○ Known Personally	Issued By:
○ Jurat	○ Passport	
○ Other:	○ Other:	Issued Date: Expiration Date:

Document Type:	Date/Time Notarized: AM PM	Document Date:	Fee Charged:

Printed Name and Address of Witness:	Phone Number:
	Email:
	Witness' Signature:

Comments:	Record Number:
	73

NOTARY RECORD

Printed Name and Address of Signer:	Phone Number:	Thumb Print:
	Email:	
	Signer's Signature:	

Service Performed:	Identification:	I.D. Number:
○ Oath	○ I.D. Card ○ Credible Witness	
○ Acknowledgment	○ Drivers License ○ Known Personally	Issued By:
○ Jurat	○ Passport	
○ Other:	○ Other:	Issued Date: Expiration Date:

Document Type:	Date/Time Notarized: AM PM	Document Date:	Fee Charged:

Printed Name and Address of Witness:	Phone Number:
	Email:
	Witness' Signature:

Comments:	Record Number:
	74

NOTARY RECORD

Printed Name and Address of Signer:	Phone Number:	Thumb Print:
	Email:	
	Signer's Signature:	

Service Performed:	Identification:	I.D. Number:	
O Oath	O I.D. Card O Credible Witness		
O Acknowledgment	O Drivers License O Known Personally	Issued By:	
O Jurat	O Passport	Issued Date:	Expiration Date:
O Other:	O Other:		
Document Type:	Date/Time Notarized: AM PM	Document Date:	Fee Charged:

Printed Name and Address of Witness:	Phone Number:
	Email:
	Witness' Signature:

Comments:	Record Number: **75**

NOTARY RECORD

Printed Name and Address of Signer:	Phone Number:	Thumb Print:
	Email:	
	Signer's Signature:	

Service Performed:	Identification:	I.D. Number:	
O Oath	O I.D. Card O Credible Witness		
O Acknowledgment	O Drivers License O Known Personally	Issued By:	
O Jurat	O Passport	Issued Date:	Expiration Date:
O Other:	O Other:		
Document Type:	Date/Time Notarized: AM PM	Document Date:	Fee Charged:

Printed Name and Address of Witness:	Phone Number:
	Email:
	Witness' Signature:

Comments:	Record Number: **76**

NOTARY RECORD

Printed Name and Address of Signer:

Phone Number:

Email:

Signer's Signature:

Thumb Print:

Service Performed:
- ○ Oath
- ○ Acknowledgment
- ○ Jurat
- ○ Other:

Identification:
- ○ I.D. Card
- ○ Drivers License
- ○ Passport
- ○ Other:
- ○ Credible Witness
- ○ Known Personally

I.D. Number:

Issued By:

Issued Date:

Expiration Date:

Document Type:

Date/Time Notarized: AM PM

Document Date:

Fee Charged:

Printed Name and Address of Witness:

Phone Number:

Email:

Witness' Signature:

Comments:

Record Number:
77

NOTARY RECORD

Printed Name and Address of Signer:

Phone Number:

Email:

Signer's Signature:

Thumb Print:

Service Performed:
- ○ Oath
- ○ Acknowledgment
- ○ Jurat
- ○ Other:

Identification:
- ○ I.D. Card
- ○ Drivers License
- ○ Passport
- ○ Other:
- ○ Credible Witness
- ○ Known Personally

I.D. Number:

Issued By:

Issued Date:

Expiration Date:

Document Type:

Date/Time Notarized: AM PM

Document Date:

Fee Charged:

Printed Name and Address of Witness:

Phone Number:

Email:

Witness' Signature:

Comments:

Record Number:
78

NOTARY RECORD

Printed Name and Address of Signer:	Phone Number:	Thumb Print:
	Email:	
	Signer's Signature:	

Service Performed:	Identification:	I.D. Number:	
O Oath	O I.D. Card O Credible Witness		
O Acknowledgment	O Drivers License O Known Personally	Issued By:	
O Jurat	O Passport	Issued Date:	Expiration Date:
O Other:	O Other:		
Document Type:	Date/Time Notarized: AM PM	Document Date:	Fee Charged:

Printed Name and Address of Witness:	Phone Number:
	Email:
	Witness' Signature:

Comments:	Record Number: **79**

NOTARY RECORD

Printed Name and Address of Signer:	Phone Number:	Thumb Print:
	Email:	
	Signer's Signature:	

Service Performed:	Identification:	I.D. Number:	
O Oath	O I.D. Card O Credible Witness		
O Acknowledgment	O Drivers License O Known Personally	Issued By:	
O Jurat	O Passport	Issued Date:	Expiration Date:
O Other:	O Other:		
Document Type:	Date/Time Notarized: AM PM	Document Date:	Fee Charged:

Printed Name and Address of Witness:	Phone Number:
	Email:
	Witness' Signature:

Comments:	Record Number: **80**

NOTARY RECORD

Printed Name and Address of Signer:

Phone Number:

Email:

Signer's Signature:

Thumb Print:

Service Performed:
- ○ Oath
- ○ Acknowledgment
- ○ Jurat
- ○ Other:

Identification:
- ○ I.D. Card
- ○ Drivers License
- ○ Passport
- ○ Other:
- ○ Credible Witness
- ○ Known Personally

I.D. Number:

Issued By:

Issued Date:

Expiration Date:

Document Type:

Date/Time Notarized: AM PM

Document Date:

Fee Charged:

Printed Name and Address of Witness:

Phone Number:

Email:

Witness' Signature:

Comments:

Record Number:
81

NOTARY RECORD

Printed Name and Address of Signer:

Phone Number:

Email:

Signer's Signature:

Thumb Print:

Service Performed:
- ○ Oath
- ○ Acknowledgment
- ○ Jurat
- ○ Other:

Identification:
- ○ I.D. Card
- ○ Drivers License
- ○ Passport
- ○ Other:
- ○ Credible Witness
- ○ Known Personally

I.D. Number:

Issued By:

Issued Date:

Expiration Date:

Document Type:

Date/Time Notarized: AM PM

Document Date:

Fee Charged:

Printed Name and Address of Witness:

Phone Number:

Email:

Witness' Signature:

Comments:

Record Number:
82

NOTARY RECORD

Printed Name and Address of Signer:	**Phone Number:**	**Thumb Print:**
	Email:	
	Signer's Signature:	

Service Performed:	**Identification:**	**I.D. Number:**	
O Oath	O I.D. Card O Credible Witness		
O Acknowledgment	O Drivers License O Known Personally	**Issued By:**	
O Jurat	O Passport	**Issued Date:**	**Expiration Date:**
O Other:	O Other:		
Document Type:	**Date/Time Notarized:** AM / PM	**Document Date:**	**Fee Charged:**

Printed Name and Address of Witness:	**Phone Number:**
	Email:
	Witness' Signature:

Comments:	**Record Number:** **83**

NOTARY RECORD

Printed Name and Address of Signer:	**Phone Number:**	**Thumb Print:**
	Email:	
	Signer's Signature:	

Service Performed:	**Identification:**	**I.D. Number:**	
O Oath	O I.D. Card O Credible Witness		
O Acknowledgment	O Drivers License O Known Personally	**Issued By:**	
O Jurat	O Passport	**Issued Date:**	**Expiration Date:**
O Other:	O Other:		
Document Type:	**Date/Time Notarized:** AM / PM	**Document Date:**	**Fee Charged:**

Printed Name and Address of Witness:	**Phone Number:**
	Email:
	Witness' Signature:

Comments:	**Record Number:** **84**

NOTARY RECORD

Printed Name and Address of Signer:

Phone Number:

Email:

Signer's Signature:

Thumb Print:

Service Performed:
- ○ Oath
- ○ Acknowledgment
- ○ Jurat
- ○ Other:

Identification:
- ○ I.D. Card
- ○ Drivers License
- ○ Passport
- ○ Other:
- ○ Credible Witness
- ○ Known Personally

I.D. Number:

Issued By:

Issued Date:

Expiration Date:

Document Type:

Date/Time Notarized: AM PM

Document Date:

Fee Charged:

Printed Name and Address of Witness:

Phone Number:

Email:

Witness' Signature:

Comments:

Record Number: 85

NOTARY RECORD

Printed Name and Address of Signer:

Phone Number:

Email:

Signer's Signature:

Thumb Print:

Service Performed:
- ○ Oath
- ○ Acknowledgment
- ○ Jurat
- ○ Other:

Identification:
- ○ I.D. Card
- ○ Drivers License
- ○ Passport
- ○ Other:
- ○ Credible Witness
- ○ Known Personally

I.D. Number:

Issued By:

Issued Date:

Expiration Date:

Document Type:

Date/Time Notarized: AM PM

Document Date:

Fee Charged:

Printed Name and Address of Witness:

Phone Number:

Email:

Witness' Signature:

Comments:

Record Number: 86

NOTARY RECORD

Printed Name and Address of Signer:	Phone Number:	Thumb Print:
	Email:	
	Signer's Signature:	

Service Performed:	Identification:	I.D. Number:
O Oath	O I.D. Card O Credible Witness	
O Acknowledgment	O Drivers License O Known Personally	Issued By:
O Jurat	O Passport	Issued Date: / Expiration Date:
O Other:	O Other:	

Document Type:	Date/Time Notarized: AM / PM	Document Date:	Fee Charged:

Printed Name and Address of Witness:	Phone Number:
	Email:
	Witness' Signature:

Comments:	Record Number: **87**

NOTARY RECORD

Printed Name and Address of Signer:	Phone Number:	Thumb Print:
	Email:	
	Signer's Signature:	

Service Performed:	Identification:	I.D. Number:
O Oath	O I.D. Card O Credible Witness	
O Acknowledgment	O Drivers License O Known Personally	Issued By:
O Jurat	O Passport	Issued Date: / Expiration Date:
O Other:	O Other:	

Document Type:	Date/Time Notarized: AM / PM	Document Date:	Fee Charged:

Printed Name and Address of Witness:	Phone Number:
	Email:
	Witness' Signature:

Comments:	Record Number: **88**

NOTARY RECORD

Printed Name and Address of Signer:

Phone Number:

Email:

Signer's Signature:

Thumb Print:

Service Performed:
- ○ Oath
- ○ Acknowledgment
- ○ Jurat
- ○ Other:

Identification:
- ○ I.D. Card   ○ Credible Witness
- ○ Drivers License   ○ Known Personally
- ○ Passport
- ○ Other:

I.D. Number:

Issued By:

Issued Date:

Expiration Date:

Document Type:

Date/Time Notarized: AM   PM

Document Date:

Fee Charged:

Printed Name and Address of Witness:

Phone Number:

Email:

Witness' Signature:

Comments:

Record Number:
89

NOTARY RECORD

Printed Name and Address of Signer:

Phone Number:

Email:

Signer's Signature:

Thumb Print:

Service Performed:
- ○ Oath
- ○ Acknowledgment
- ○ Jurat
- ○ Other:

Identification:
- ○ I.D. Card   ○ Credible Witness
- ○ Drivers License   ○ Known Personally
- ○ Passport
- ○ Other:

I.D. Number:

Issued By:

Issued Date:

Expiration Date:

Document Type:

Date/Time Notarized: AM   PM

Document Date:

Fee Charged:

Printed Name and Address of Witness:

Phone Number:

Email:

Witness' Signature:

Comments:

Record Number:
90

NOTARY RECORD

Printed Name and Address of Signer:	Phone Number:	Thumb Print:
	Email:	
	Signer's Signature:	

Service Performed:	Identification:	I.D. Number:
O Oath	O I.D. Card O Credible Witness	
O Acknowledgment	O Drivers License O Known Personally	Issued By:
O Jurat	O Passport	
O Other:	O Other:	Issued Date: Expiration Date:
Document Type:	Date/Time Notarized: AM PM	Document Date: Fee Charged:

Printed Name and Address of Witness:	Phone Number:
	Email:
	Witness' Signature:

Comments:	Record Number: **91**

NOTARY RECORD

Printed Name and Address of Signer:	Phone Number:	Thumb Print:
	Email:	
	Signer's Signature:	

Service Performed:	Identification:	I.D. Number:
O Oath	O I.D. Card O Credible Witness	
O Acknowledgment	O Drivers License O Known Personally	Issued By:
O Jurat	O Passport	
O Other:	O Other:	Issued Date: Expiration Date:
Document Type:	Date/Time Notarized: AM PM	Document Date: Fee Charged:

Printed Name and Address of Witness:	Phone Number:
	Email:
	Witness' Signature:

Comments:	Record Number: **92**

NOTARY RECORD

Printed Name and Address of Signer:

Phone Number:

Email:

Signer's Signature:

Thumb Print:

Service Performed:
- ○ Oath
- ○ Acknowledgment
- ○ Jurat
- ○ Other:

Identification:
- ○ I.D. Card
- ○ Drivers License
- ○ Passport
- ○ Other:
- ○ Credible Witness
- ○ Known Personally

I.D. Number:

Issued By:

Issued Date:

Expiration Date:

Document Type:

Date/Time Notarized: AM PM

Document Date:

Fee Charged:

Printed Name and Address of Witness:

Phone Number:

Email:

Witness' Signature:

Comments:

Record Number:
93

NOTARY RECORD

Printed Name and Address of Signer:

Phone Number:

Email:

Signer's Signature:

Thumb Print:

Service Performed:
- ○ Oath
- ○ Acknowledgment
- ○ Jurat
- ○ Other:

Identification:
- ○ I.D. Card
- ○ Drivers License
- ○ Passport
- ○ Other:
- ○ Credible Witness
- ○ Known Personally

I.D. Number:

Issued By:

Issued Date:

Expiration Date:

Document Type:

Date/Time Notarized: AM PM

Document Date:

Fee Charged:

Printed Name and Address of Witness:

Phone Number:

Email:

Witness' Signature:

Comments:

Record Number:
94

NOTARY RECORD

Printed Name and Address of Signer:	Phone Number:	Thumb Print:
	Email:	
	Signer's Signature:	

Service Performed:	Identification:	I.D. Number:
○ Oath	○ I.D. Card ○ Credible Witness	
○ Acknowledgment	○ Drivers License ○ Known Personally	Issued By:
○ Jurat	○ Passport	
○ Other:	○ Other:	Issued Date: Expiration Date:

Document Type:	Date/Time Notarized: AM PM	Document Date: Fee Charged:

Printed Name and Address of Witness:	Phone Number:
	Email:
	Witness' Signature:

Comments:	Record Number: **95**

NOTARY RECORD

Printed Name and Address of Signer:	Phone Number:	Thumb Print:
	Email:	
	Signer's Signature:	

Service Performed:	Identification:	I.D. Number:
○ Oath	○ I.D. Card ○ Credible Witness	
○ Acknowledgment	○ Drivers License ○ Known Personally	Issued By:
○ Jurat	○ Passport	
○ Other:	○ Other:	Issued Date: Expiration Date:

Document Type:	Date/Time Notarized: AM PM	Document Date: Fee Charged:

Printed Name and Address of Witness:	Phone Number:
	Email:
	Witness' Signature:

Comments:	Record Number: **96**

NOTARY RECORD

Printed Name and Address of Signer:

Phone Number:

Email:

Signer's Signature:

Thumb Print:

Service Performed:
- ○ Oath
- ○ Acknowledgment
- ○ Jurat
- ○ Other:

Identification:
- ○ I.D. Card
- ○ Drivers License
- ○ Passport
- ○ Other:
- ○ Credible Witness
- ○ Known Personally

I.D. Number:

Issued By:

Issued Date:

Expiration Date:

Document Type:

Date/Time Notarized: AM / PM

Document Date:

Fee Charged:

Printed Name and Address of Witness:

Phone Number:

Email:

Witness' Signature:

Comments:

Record Number:
97

NOTARY RECORD

Printed Name and Address of Signer:

Phone Number:

Email:

Signer's Signature:

Thumb Print:

Service Performed:
- ○ Oath
- ○ Acknowledgment
- ○ Jurat
- ○ Other:

Identification:
- ○ I.D. Card
- ○ Drivers License
- ○ Passport
- ○ Other:
- ○ Credible Witness
- ○ Known Personally

I.D. Number:

Issued By:

Issued Date:

Expiration Date:

Document Type:

Date/Time Notarized: AM / PM

Document Date:

Fee Charged:

Printed Name and Address of Witness:

Phone Number:

Email:

Witness' Signature:

Comments:

Record Number:
98

NOTARY RECORD

Printed Name and Address of Signer:

Phone Number:

Email:

Signer's Signature:

Thumb Print:

Service Performed:
- ○ Oath
- ○ Acknowledgment
- ○ Jurat
- ○ Other:

Identification:
- ○ I.D. Card
- ○ Drivers License
- ○ Passport
- ○ Other:
- ○ Credible Witness
- ○ Known Personally

I.D. Number:

Issued By:

Issued Date:

Expiration Date:

Document Type:

Date/Time Notarized: AM PM

Document Date:

Fee Charged:

Printed Name and Address of Witness:

Phone Number:

Email:

Witness' Signature:

Comments:

Record Number:
99

NOTARY RECORD

Printed Name and Address of Signer:

Phone Number:

Email:

Signer's Signature:

Thumb Print:

Service Performed:
- ○ Oath
- ○ Acknowledgment
- ○ Jurat
- ○ Other:

Identification:
- ○ I.D. Card
- ○ Drivers License
- ○ Passport
- ○ Other:
- ○ Credible Witness
- ○ Known Personally

I.D. Number:

Issued By:

Issued Date:

Expiration Date:

Document Type:

Date/Time Notarized: AM PM

Document Date:

Fee Charged:

Printed Name and Address of Witness:

Phone Number:

Email:

Witness' Signature:

Comments:

Record Number:
100

NOTARY RECORD

Printed Name and Address of Signer:	Phone Number:	Thumb Print:
	Email:	
	Signer's Signature:	

Service Performed:	Identification:	I.D. Number:
O Oath	O I.D. Card O Credible Witness	
O Acknowledgment	O Drivers License O Known Personally	Issued By:
O Jurat	O Passport	
O Other:	O Other:	Issued Date: Expiration Date:

Document Type:	Date/Time Notarized: AM / PM	Document Date:	Fee Charged:

Printed Name and Address of Witness:	Phone Number:
	Email:
	Witness' Signature:

Comments:	Record Number: **101**

NOTARY RECORD

Printed Name and Address of Signer:	Phone Number:	Thumb Print:
	Email:	
	Signer's Signature:	

Service Performed:	Identification:	I.D. Number:
O Oath	O I.D. Card O Credible Witness	
O Acknowledgment	O Drivers License O Known Personally	Issued By:
O Jurat	O Passport	
O Other:	O Other:	Issued Date: Expiration Date:

Document Type:	Date/Time Notarized: AM / PM	Document Date:	Fee Charged:

Printed Name and Address of Witness:	Phone Number:
	Email:
	Witness' Signature:

Comments:	Record Number: **102**

NOTARY RECORD

Printed Name and Address of Signer:	Phone Number:		Thumb Print:
	Email:		
	Signer's Signature:		

Service Performed:	Identification:		I.D. Number:	
○ Oath	○ I.D. Card	○ Credible Witness		
○ Acknowledgment	○ Drivers License	○ Known Personally	Issued By:	
○ Jurat	○ Passport		Issued Date:	Expiration Date:
○ Other:	○ Other:			
Document Type:	Date/Time Notarized:	AM PM	Document Date:	Fee Charged:

Printed Name and Address of Witness:	Phone Number:
	Email:
	Witness' Signature:

Comments:	Record Number: **103**

NOTARY RECORD

Printed Name and Address of Signer:	Phone Number:		Thumb Print:
	Email:		
	Signer's Signature:		

Service Performed:	Identification:		I.D. Number:	
○ Oath	○ I.D. Card	○ Credible Witness		
○ Acknowledgment	○ Drivers License	○ Known Personally	Issued By:	
○ Jurat	○ Passport		Issued Date:	Expiration Date:
○ Other:	○ Other:			
Document Type:	Date/Time Notarized:	AM PM	Document Date:	Fee Charged:

Printed Name and Address of Witness:	Phone Number:
	Email:
	Witness' Signature:

Comments:	Record Number: **104**

NOTARY RECORD

Printed Name and Address of Signer:

Phone Number:

Email:

Signer's Signature:

Thumb Print:

Service Performed:
- ○ Oath
- ○ Acknowledgment
- ○ Jurat
- ○ Other:

Identification:
- ○ I.D. Card
- ○ Drivers License
- ○ Passport
- ○ Other:
- ○ Credible Witness
- ○ Known Personally

I.D. Number:

Issued By:

Issued Date:

Expiration Date:

Document Type:

Date/Time Notarized: AM PM

Document Date:

Fee Charged:

Printed Name and Address of Witness:

Phone Number:

Email:

Witness' Signature:

Comments:

Record Number: 105

NOTARY RECORD

Printed Name and Address of Signer:

Phone Number:

Email:

Signer's Signature:

Thumb Print:

Service Performed:
- ○ Oath
- ○ Acknowledgment
- ○ Jurat
- ○ Other:

Identification:
- ○ I.D. Card
- ○ Drivers License
- ○ Passport
- ○ Other:
- ○ Credible Witness
- ○ Known Personally

I.D. Number:

Issued By:

Issued Date:

Expiration Date:

Document Type:

Date/Time Notarized: AM PM

Document Date:

Fee Charged:

Printed Name and Address of Witness:

Phone Number:

Email:

Witness' Signature:

Comments:

Record Number: 106

NOTARY RECORD

Printed Name and Address of Signer:

Phone Number:

Email:

Signer's Signature:

Thumb Print:

Service Performed:
- ○ Oath
- ○ Acknowledgment
- ○ Jurat
- ○ Other:

Identification:
- ○ I.D. Card
- ○ Drivers License
- ○ Passport
- ○ Other:
- ○ Credible Witness
- ○ Known Personally

I.D. Number:

Issued By:

Issued Date:

Expiration Date:

Document Type:

Date/Time Notarized: AM PM

Document Date:

Fee Charged:

Printed Name and Address of Witness:

Phone Number:

Email:

Witness' Signature:

Comments:

Record Number: 107

NOTARY RECORD

Printed Name and Address of Signer:

Phone Number:

Email:

Signer's Signature:

Thumb Print:

Service Performed:
- ○ Oath
- ○ Acknowledgment
- ○ Jurat
- ○ Other:

Identification:
- ○ I.D. Card
- ○ Drivers License
- ○ Passport
- ○ Other:
- ○ Credible Witness
- ○ Known Personally

I.D. Number:

Issued By:

Issued Date:

Expiration Date:

Document Type:

Date/Time Notarized: AM PM

Document Date:

Fee Charged:

Printed Name and Address of Witness:

Phone Number:

Email:

Witness' Signature:

Comments:

Record Number: 108

NOTARY RECORD

Printed Name and Address of Signer:

Phone Number:

Email:

Signer's Signature:

Thumb Print:

Service Performed:
- ○ Oath
- ○ Acknowledgment
- ○ Jurat
- ○ Other:

Identification:
- ○ I.D. Card
- ○ Drivers License
- ○ Passport
- ○ Other:
- ○ Credible Witness
- ○ Known Personally

I.D. Number:

Issued By:

Issued Date:

Expiration Date:

Document Type:

Date/Time Notarized: AM PM

Document Date:

Fee Charged:

Printed Name and Address of Witness:

Phone Number:

Email:

Witness' Signature:

Comments:

Record Number:
109

NOTARY RECORD

Printed Name and Address of Signer:

Phone Number:

Email:

Signer's Signature:

Thumb Print:

Service Performed:
- ○ Oath
- ○ Acknowledgment
- ○ Jurat
- ○ Other:

Identification:
- ○ I.D. Card
- ○ Drivers License
- ○ Passport
- ○ Other:
- ○ Credible Witness
- ○ Known Personally

I.D. Number:

Issued By:

Issued Date:

Expiration Date:

Document Type:

Date/Time Notarized: AM PM

Document Date:

Fee Charged:

Printed Name and Address of Witness:

Phone Number:

Email:

Witness' Signature:

Comments:

Record Number:
110

NOTARY RECORD

Printed Name and Address of Signer:	Phone Number:	Thumb Print:
	Email:	
	Signer's Signature:	

Service Performed:
- ○ Oath
- ○ Acknowledgment
- ○ Jurat
- ○ Other:

Identification:
- ○ I.D. Card   ○ Credible Witness
- ○ Drivers License   ○ Known Personally
- ○ Passport
- ○ Other:

I.D. Number:

Issued By:

Issued Date:	Expiration Date:

Document Type:	Date/Time Notarized: AM PM	Document Date:	Fee Charged:

Printed Name and Address of Witness:	Phone Number:
	Email:
	Witness' Signature:

Comments:

Record Number: 111

NOTARY RECORD

Printed Name and Address of Signer:	Phone Number:	Thumb Print:
	Email:	
	Signer's Signature:	

Service Performed:
- ○ Oath
- ○ Acknowledgment
- ○ Jurat
- ○ Other:

Identification:
- ○ I.D. Card   ○ Credible Witness
- ○ Drivers License   ○ Known Personally
- ○ Passport
- ○ Other:

I.D. Number:

Issued By:

Issued Date:	Expiration Date:

Document Type:	Date/Time Notarized: AM PM	Document Date:	Fee Charged:

Printed Name and Address of Witness:	Phone Number:
	Email:
	Witness' Signature:

Comments:

Record Number: 112

NOTARY RECORD

Printed Name and Address of Signer:	Phone Number:	Thumb Print:
	Email:	
	Signer's Signature:	

Service Performed:	Identification:	I.D. Number:	
O Oath	O I.D. Card O Credible Witness		
O Acknowledgment	O Drivers License O Known Personally	Issued By:	
O Jurat	O Passport		
O Other:	O Other:	Issued Date:	Expiration Date:
Document Type:	Date/Time Notarized: AM PM	Document Date:	Fee Charged:

Printed Name and Address of Witness:	Phone Number:
	Email:
	Witness' Signature:

Comments:	Record Number: **113**

NOTARY RECORD

Printed Name and Address of Signer:	Phone Number:	Thumb Print:
	Email:	
	Signer's Signature:	

Service Performed:	Identification:	I.D. Number:	
O Oath	O I.D. Card O Credible Witness		
O Acknowledgment	O Drivers License O Known Personally	Issued By:	
O Jurat	O Passport		
O Other:	O Other:	Issued Date:	Expiration Date:
Document Type:	Date/Time Notarized: AM PM	Document Date:	Fee Charged:

Printed Name and Address of Witness:	Phone Number:
	Email:
	Witness' Signature:

Comments:	Record Number: **114**

NOTARY RECORD

Printed Name and Address of Signer:	Phone Number:	Thumb Print:
	Email:	
	Signer's Signature:	

Service Performed:	Identification:	I.D. Number:	
○ Oath	○ I.D. Card ○ Credible Witness		
○ Acknowledgment	○ Drivers License ○ Known Personally	Issued By:	
○ Jurat	○ Passport		
○ Other:	○ Other:	Issued Date:	Expiration Date:
Document Type:	Date/Time Notarized: AM PM	Document Date:	Fee Charged:

Printed Name and Address of Witness:	Phone Number:
	Email:
	Witness' Signature:

Comments:	Record Number: **115**

NOTARY RECORD

Printed Name and Address of Signer:	Phone Number:	Thumb Print:
	Email:	
	Signer's Signature:	

Service Performed:	Identification:	I.D. Number:	
○ Oath	○ I.D. Card ○ Credible Witness		
○ Acknowledgment	○ Drivers License ○ Known Personally	Issued By:	
○ Jurat	○ Passport		
○ Other:	○ Other:	Issued Date:	Expiration Date:
Document Type:	Date/Time Notarized: AM PM	Document Date:	Fee Charged:

Printed Name and Address of Witness:	Phone Number:
	Email:
	Witness' Signature:

Comments:	Record Number: **116**

NOTARY RECORD

Printed Name and Address of Signer:	Phone Number:	Thumb Print:
	Email:	
	Signer's Signature:	

Service Performed:	Identification:		I.D. Number:	
○ Oath	○ I.D. Card	○ Credible Witness		
○ Acknowledgment	○ Drivers License	○ Known Personally	Issued By:	
○ Jurat	○ Passport		Issued Date:	Expiration Date:
○ Other:	○ Other:			
Document Type:	Date/Time Notarized:	AM PM	Document Date:	Fee Charged:

Printed Name and Address of Witness:	Phone Number:
	Email:
	Witness' Signature:

Comments:	Record Number: **117**

NOTARY RECORD

Printed Name and Address of Signer:	Phone Number:	Thumb Print:
	Email:	
	Signer's Signature:	

Service Performed:	Identification:		I.D. Number:	
○ Oath	○ I.D. Card	○ Credible Witness		
○ Acknowledgment	○ Drivers License	○ Known Personally	Issued By:	
○ Jurat	○ Passport		Issued Date:	Expiration Date:
○ Other:	○ Other:			
Document Type:	Date/Time Notarized:	AM PM	Document Date:	Fee Charged:

Printed Name and Address of Witness:	Phone Number:
	Email:
	Witness' Signature:

Comments:	Record Number: **118**

NOTARY RECORD

Printed Name and Address of Signer:

Phone Number:

Email:

Signer's Signature:

Thumb Print:

Service Performed:
- ○ Oath
- ○ Acknowledgment
- ○ Jurat
- ○ Other:

Identification:
- ○ I.D. Card
- ○ Drivers License
- ○ Passport
- ○ Other:
- ○ Credible Witness
- ○ Known Personally

I.D. Number:

Issued By:

Issued Date:

Expiration Date:

Document Type:

Date/Time Notarized: AM PM

Document Date:

Fee Charged:

Printed Name and Address of Witness:

Phone Number:

Email:

Witness' Signature:

Comments:

Record Number: 119

NOTARY RECORD

Printed Name and Address of Signer:

Phone Number:

Email:

Signer's Signature:

Thumb Print:

Service Performed:
- ○ Oath
- ○ Acknowledgment
- ○ Jurat
- ○ Other:

Identification:
- ○ I.D. Card
- ○ Drivers License
- ○ Passport
- ○ Other:
- ○ Credible Witness
- ○ Known Personally

I.D. Number:

Issued By:

Issued Date:

Expiration Date:

Document Type:

Date/Time Notarized: AM PM

Document Date:

Fee Charged:

Printed Name and Address of Witness:

Phone Number:

Email:

Witness' Signature:

Comments:

Record Number: 120

NOTARY RECORD

Printed Name and Address of Signer:

Phone Number:

Email:

Signer's Signature:

Thumb Print:

Service Performed:
- ○ Oath
- ○ Acknowledgment
- ○ Jurat
- ○ Other:

Identification:
- ○ I.D. Card   ○ Credible Witness
- ○ Drivers License   ○ Known Personally
- ○ Passport
- ○ Other:

I.D. Number:

Issued By:

Issued Date:

Expiration Date:

Document Type:

Date/Time Notarized: AM   PM

Document Date:

Fee Charged:

Printed Name and Address of Witness:

Phone Number:

Email:

Witness' Signature:

Comments:

Record Number:
121

NOTARY RECORD

Printed Name and Address of Signer:

Phone Number:

Email:

Signer's Signature:

Thumb Print:

Service Performed:
- ○ Oath
- ○ Acknowledgment
- ○ Jurat
- ○ Other:

Identification:
- ○ I.D. Card   ○ Credible Witness
- ○ Drivers License   ○ Known Personally
- ○ Passport
- ○ Other:

I.D. Number:

Issued By:

Issued Date:

Expiration Date:

Document Type:

Date/Time Notarized: AM   PM

Document Date:

Fee Charged:

Printed Name and Address of Witness:

Phone Number:

Email:

Witness' Signature:

Comments:

Record Number:
122

NOTARY RECORD

Printed Name and Address of Signer:	**Phone Number:**	**Thumb Print:**
	Email:	
	Signer's Signature:	

Service Performed:
O Oath
O Acknowledgment
O Jurat
O Other:

Identification:
O I.D. Card   O Credible Witness
O Drivers License   O Known Personally
O Passport
O Other:

I.D. Number:

Issued By:

Issued Date: **Expiration Date:**

Document Type: **Date/Time Notarized:** AM PM   **Document Date:**   **Fee Charged:**

Printed Name and Address of Witness: **Phone Number:**
Email:
Witness' Signature:

Comments: **Record Number: 123**

NOTARY RECORD

Printed Name and Address of Signer:	**Phone Number:**	**Thumb Print:**
	Email:	
	Signer's Signature:	

Service Performed:
O Oath
O Acknowledgment
O Jurat
O Other:

Identification:
O I.D. Card   O Credible Witness
O Drivers License   O Known Personally
O Passport
O Other:

I.D. Number:

Issued By:

Issued Date: **Expiration Date:**

Document Type: **Date/Time Notarized:** AM PM   **Document Date:**   **Fee Charged:**

Printed Name and Address of Witness: **Phone Number:**
Email:
Witness' Signature:

Comments: **Record Number: 124**

NOTARY RECORD

Printed Name and Address of Signer:	Phone Number:	Thumb Print:
	Email:	
	Signer's Signature:	

Service Performed:
- ○ Oath
- ○ Acknowledgment
- ○ Jurat
- ○ Other:

Identification:
- ○ I.D. Card   ○ Credible Witness
- ○ Drivers License   ○ Known Personally
- ○ Passport
- ○ Other:

I.D. Number:	
Issued By:	
Issued Date:	Expiration Date:

Document Type:	Date/Time Notarized: AM PM	Document Date:	Fee Charged:

Printed Name and Address of Witness:	Phone Number:
	Email:
	Witness' Signature:

Comments:	Record Number: **125**

NOTARY RECORD

Printed Name and Address of Signer:	Phone Number:	Thumb Print:
	Email:	
	Signer's Signature:	

Service Performed:
- ○ Oath
- ○ Acknowledgment
- ○ Jurat
- ○ Other:

Identification:
- ○ I.D. Card   ○ Credible Witness
- ○ Drivers License   ○ Known Personally
- ○ Passport
- ○ Other:

I.D. Number:	
Issued By:	
Issued Date:	Expiration Date:

Document Type:	Date/Time Notarized: AM PM	Document Date:	Fee Charged:

Printed Name and Address of Witness:	Phone Number:
	Email:
	Witness' Signature:

Comments:	Record Number: **126**

NOTARY RECORD

Printed Name and Address of Signer:

Phone Number:

Email:

Signer's Signature:

Thumb Print:

Service Performed:
- ○ Oath
- ○ Acknowledgment
- ○ Jurat
- ○ Other:

Identification:
- ○ I.D. Card
- ○ Drivers License
- ○ Passport
- ○ Other:
- ○ Credible Witness
- ○ Known Personally

I.D. Number:

Issued By:

Issued Date:

Expiration Date:

Document Type:

Date/Time Notarized: AM PM

Document Date:

Fee Charged:

Printed Name and Address of Witness:

Phone Number:

Email:

Witness' Signature:

Comments:

Record Number: 127

NOTARY RECORD

Printed Name and Address of Signer:

Phone Number:

Email:

Signer's Signature:

Thumb Print:

Service Performed:
- ○ Oath
- ○ Acknowledgment
- ○ Jurat
- ○ Other:

Identification:
- ○ I.D. Card
- ○ Drivers License
- ○ Passport
- ○ Other:
- ○ Credible Witness
- ○ Known Personally

I.D. Number:

Issued By:

Issued Date:

Expiration Date:

Document Type:

Date/Time Notarized: AM PM

Document Date:

Fee Charged:

Printed Name and Address of Witness:

Phone Number:

Email:

Witness' Signature:

Comments:

Record Number: 128

NOTARY RECORD

Printed Name and Address of Signer:

Phone Number:

Email:

Signer's Signature:

Thumb Print:

Service Performed:
- ○ Oath
- ○ Acknowledgment
- ○ Jurat
- ○ Other:

Identification:
- ○ I.D. Card   ○ Credible Witness
- ○ Drivers License   ○ Known Personally
- ○ Passport
- ○ Other:

I.D. Number:

Issued By:

Issued Date:

Expiration Date:

Document Type:

Date/Time Notarized: AM / PM

Document Date:

Fee Charged:

Printed Name and Address of Witness:

Phone Number:

Email:

Witness' Signature:

Comments:

Record Number:
129

NOTARY RECORD

Printed Name and Address of Signer:

Phone Number:

Email:

Signer's Signature:

Thumb Print:

Service Performed:
- ○ Oath
- ○ Acknowledgment
- ○ Jurat
- ○ Other:

Identification:
- ○ I.D. Card   ○ Credible Witness
- ○ Drivers License   ○ Known Personally
- ○ Passport
- ○ Other:

I.D. Number:

Issued By:

Issued Date:

Expiration Date:

Document Type:

Date/Time Notarized: AM / PM

Document Date:

Fee Charged:

Printed Name and Address of Witness:

Phone Number:

Email:

Witness' Signature:

Comments:

Record Number:
130

NOTARY RECORD

Printed Name and Address of Signer:

Phone Number:

Email:

Signer's Signature:

Thumb Print:

Service Performed:
- ○ Oath
- ○ Acknowledgment
- ○ Jurat
- ○ Other:

Identification:
- ○ I.D. Card
- ○ Drivers License
- ○ Passport
- ○ Other:
- ○ Credible Witness
- ○ Known Personally

I.D. Number:

Issued By:

Issued Date:

Expiration Date:

Document Type:

Date/Time Notarized: AM PM

Document Date:

Fee Charged:

Printed Name and Address of Witness:

Phone Number:

Email:

Witness' Signature:

Comments:

Record Number: 131

NOTARY RECORD

Printed Name and Address of Signer:

Phone Number:

Email:

Signer's Signature:

Thumb Print:

Service Performed:
- ○ Oath
- ○ Acknowledgment
- ○ Jurat
- ○ Other:

Identification:
- ○ I.D. Card
- ○ Drivers License
- ○ Passport
- ○ Other:
- ○ Credible Witness
- ○ Known Personally

I.D. Number:

Issued By:

Issued Date:

Expiration Date:

Document Type:

Date/Time Notarized: AM PM

Document Date:

Fee Charged:

Printed Name and Address of Witness:

Phone Number:

Email:

Witness' Signature:

Comments:

Record Number: 132

NOTARY RECORD

Printed Name and Address of Signer:

Phone Number:

Email:

Signer's Signature:

Thumb Print:

Service Performed:
- ○ Oath
- ○ Acknowledgment
- ○ Jurat
- ○ Other:

Identification:
- ○ I.D. Card   ○ Credible Witness
- ○ Drivers License ○ Known Personally
- ○ Passport
- ○ Other:

I.D. Number:

Issued By:

Issued Date: | **Expiration Date:**

Document Type: | **Date/Time Notarized:** AM PM | **Document Date:** | **Fee Charged:**

Printed Name and Address of Witness:

Phone Number:

Email:

Witness' Signature:

Comments:

Record Number: 133

NOTARY RECORD

Printed Name and Address of Signer:

Phone Number:

Email:

Signer's Signature:

Thumb Print:

Service Performed:
- ○ Oath
- ○ Acknowledgment
- ○ Jurat
- ○ Other:

Identification:
- ○ I.D. Card   ○ Credible Witness
- ○ Drivers License ○ Known Personally
- ○ Passport
- ○ Other:

I.D. Number:

Issued By:

Issued Date: | **Expiration Date:**

Document Type: | **Date/Time Notarized:** AM PM | **Document Date:** | **Fee Charged:**

Printed Name and Address of Witness:

Phone Number:

Email:

Witness' Signature:

Comments:

Record Number: 134

NOTARY RECORD

Printed Name and Address of Signer:

Phone Number:

Email:

Signer's Signature:

Thumb Print:

Service Performed:
- ○ Oath
- ○ Acknowledgment
- ○ Jurat
- ○ Other:

Identification:
- ○ I.D. Card   ○ Credible Witness
- ○ Drivers License   ○ Known Personally
- ○ Passport
- ○ Other:

I.D. Number:

Issued By:

Issued Date:

Expiration Date:

Document Type:

Date/Time Notarized: AM PM

Document Date:

Fee Charged:

Printed Name and Address of Witness:

Phone Number:

Email:

Witness' Signature:

Comments:

Record Number:
135

NOTARY RECORD

Printed Name and Address of Signer:

Phone Number:

Email:

Signer's Signature:

Thumb Print:

Service Performed:
- ○ Oath
- ○ Acknowledgment
- ○ Jurat
- ○ Other:

Identification:
- ○ I.D. Card   ○ Credible Witness
- ○ Drivers License   ○ Known Personally
- ○ Passport
- ○ Other:

I.D. Number:

Issued By:

Issued Date:

Expiration Date:

Document Type:

Date/Time Notarized: AM PM

Document Date:

Fee Charged:

Printed Name and Address of Witness:

Phone Number:

Email:

Witness' Signature:

Comments:

Record Number:
136

NOTARY RECORD

Printed Name and Address of Signer:	Phone Number:	Thumb Print:
	Email:	
	Signer's Signature:	

Service Performed:	Identification:	I.D. Number:	
O Oath	O I.D. Card O Credible Witness		
O Acknowledgment	O Drivers License O Known Personally	Issued By:	
O Jurat	O Passport		
O Other:	O Other:	Issued Date:	Expiration Date:
Document Type:	Date/Time Notarized: AM / PM	Document Date:	Fee Charged:

Printed Name and Address of Witness:	Phone Number:
	Email:
	Witness' Signature:

Comments:	Record Number: **137**

NOTARY RECORD

Printed Name and Address of Signer:	Phone Number:	Thumb Print:
	Email:	
	Signer's Signature:	

Service Performed:	Identification:	I.D. Number:	
O Oath	O I.D. Card O Credible Witness		
O Acknowledgment	O Drivers License O Known Personally	Issued By:	
O Jurat	O Passport		
O Other:	O Other:	Issued Date:	Expiration Date:
Document Type:	Date/Time Notarized: AM / PM	Document Date:	Fee Charged:

Printed Name and Address of Witness:	Phone Number:
	Email:
	Witness' Signature:

Comments:	Record Number: **138**

NOTARY RECORD

Printed Name and Address of Signer:	Phone Number:	Thumb Print:
	Email:	
	Signer's Signature:	

Service Performed:	Identification:	I.D. Number:	
O Oath	O I.D. Card O Credible Witness		
O Acknowledgment	O Drivers License O Known Personally	Issued By:	
O Jurat	O Passport		
O Other:	O Other:	Issued Date:	Expiration Date:

Document Type:	Date/Time Notarized: AM / PM	Document Date:	Fee Charged:

Printed Name and Address of Witness:	Phone Number:
	Email:
	Witness' Signature:

Comments:	Record Number:
	139

NOTARY RECORD

Printed Name and Address of Signer:	Phone Number:	Thumb Print:
	Email:	
	Signer's Signature:	

Service Performed:	Identification:	I.D. Number:	
O Oath	O I.D. Card O Credible Witness		
O Acknowledgment	O Drivers License O Known Personally	Issued By:	
O Jurat	O Passport		
O Other:	O Other:	Issued Date:	Expiration Date:

Document Type:	Date/Time Notarized: AM / PM	Document Date:	Fee Charged:

Printed Name and Address of Witness:	Phone Number:
	Email:
	Witness' Signature:

Comments:	Record Number:
	140

NOTARY RECORD

Printed Name and Address of Signer:	**Phone Number:**	**Thumb Print:**
	Email:	
	Signer's Signature:	

Service Performed:
○ Oath
○ Acknowledgment
○ Jurat
○ Other:

Identification:
○ I.D. Card   ○ Credible Witness
○ Drivers License   ○ Known Personally
○ Passport
○ Other:

I.D. Number:

Issued By:

Issued Date: | **Expiration Date:**

Document Type: | **Date/Time Notarized:** AM PM | **Document Date:** | **Fee Charged:**

Printed Name and Address of Witness:	**Phone Number:**
	Email:
	Witness' Signature:

Comments: | **Record Number: 141**

NOTARY RECORD

Printed Name and Address of Signer:	**Phone Number:**	**Thumb Print:**
	Email:	
	Signer's Signature:	

Service Performed:
○ Oath
○ Acknowledgment
○ Jurat
○ Other:

Identification:
○ I.D. Card   ○ Credible Witness
○ Drivers License   ○ Known Personally
○ Passport
○ Other:

I.D. Number:

Issued By:

Issued Date: | **Expiration Date:**

Document Type: | **Date/Time Notarized:** AM PM | **Document Date:** | **Fee Charged:**

Printed Name and Address of Witness:	**Phone Number:**
	Email:
	Witness' Signature:

Comments: | **Record Number: 142**

NOTARY RECORD

Printed Name and Address of Signer:	Phone Number:	Thumb Print:
	Email:	
	Signer's Signature:	

Service Performed:	Identification:	I.D. Number:	
○ Oath	○ I.D. Card ○ Credible Witness		
○ Acknowledgment	○ Drivers License ○ Known Personally	Issued By:	
○ Jurat	○ Passport		
○ Other:	○ Other:	Issued Date:	Expiration Date:
Document Type:	Date/Time Notarized: AM PM	Document Date:	Fee Charged:

Printed Name and Address of Witness:	Phone Number:
	Email:
	Witness' Signature:

Comments:	Record Number: **143**

NOTARY RECORD

Printed Name and Address of Signer:	Phone Number:	Thumb Print:
	Email:	
	Signer's Signature:	

Service Performed:	Identification:	I.D. Number:	
○ Oath	○ I.D. Card ○ Credible Witness		
○ Acknowledgment	○ Drivers License ○ Known Personally	Issued By:	
○ Jurat	○ Passport		
○ Other:	○ Other:	Issued Date:	Expiration Date:
Document Type:	Date/Time Notarized: AM PM	Document Date:	Fee Charged:

Printed Name and Address of Witness:	Phone Number:
	Email:
	Witness' Signature:

Comments:	Record Number: **144**

NOTARY RECORD

Printed Name and Address of Signer:

Phone Number:

Email:

Signer's Signature:

Thumb Print:

Service Performed:
- ○ Oath
- ○ Acknowledgment
- ○ Jurat
- ○ Other:

Identification:
- ○ I.D. Card
- ○ Drivers License
- ○ Passport
- ○ Other:
- ○ Credible Witness
- ○ Known Personally

I.D. Number:

Issued By:

Issued Date:

Expiration Date:

Document Type:

Date/Time Notarized: AM PM

Document Date:

Fee Charged:

Printed Name and Address of Witness:

Phone Number:

Email:

Witness' Signature:

Comments:

Record Number:
145

NOTARY RECORD

Printed Name and Address of Signer:

Phone Number:

Email:

Signer's Signature:

Thumb Print:

Service Performed:
- ○ Oath
- ○ Acknowledgment
- ○ Jurat
- ○ Other:

Identification:
- ○ I.D. Card
- ○ Drivers License
- ○ Passport
- ○ Other:
- ○ Credible Witness
- ○ Known Personally

I.D. Number:

Issued By:

Issued Date:

Expiration Date:

Document Type:

Date/Time Notarized: AM PM

Document Date:

Fee Charged:

Printed Name and Address of Witness:

Phone Number:

Email:

Witness' Signature:

Comments:

Record Number:
146

NOTARY RECORD

Printed Name and Address of Signer:

Phone Number:

Email:

Signer's Signature:

Thumb Print:

Service Performed:
- ○ Oath
- ○ Acknowledgment
- ○ Jurat
- ○ Other:

Identification:
- ○ I.D. Card
- ○ Drivers License
- ○ Passport
- ○ Other:
- ○ Credible Witness
- ○ Known Personally

I.D. Number:

Issued By:

Issued Date:

Expiration Date:

Document Type:

Date/Time Notarized: AM PM

Document Date:

Fee Charged:

Printed Name and Address of Witness:

Phone Number:

Email:

Witness' Signature:

Comments:

Record Number: 147

NOTARY RECORD

Printed Name and Address of Signer:

Phone Number:

Email:

Signer's Signature:

Thumb Print:

Service Performed:
- ○ Oath
- ○ Acknowledgment
- ○ Jurat
- ○ Other:

Identification:
- ○ I.D. Card
- ○ Drivers License
- ○ Passport
- ○ Other:
- ○ Credible Witness
- ○ Known Personally

I.D. Number:

Issued By:

Issued Date:

Expiration Date:

Document Type:

Date/Time Notarized: AM PM

Document Date:

Fee Charged:

Printed Name and Address of Witness:

Phone Number:

Email:

Witness' Signature:

Comments:

Record Number: 148

NOTARY RECORD

Printed Name and Address of Signer:

Phone Number:

Email:

Signer's Signature:

Thumb Print:

Service Performed:
- ○ Oath
- ○ Acknowledgment
- ○ Jurat
- ○ Other:

Identification:
- ○ I.D. Card
- ○ Drivers License
- ○ Passport
- ○ Other:
- ○ Credible Witness
- ○ Known Personally

I.D. Number:

Issued By:

Issued Date:

Expiration Date:

Document Type:

Date/Time Notarized: AM PM

Document Date:

Fee Charged:

Printed Name and Address of Witness:

Phone Number:

Email:

Witness' Signature:

Comments:

Record Number:
149

NOTARY RECORD

Printed Name and Address of Signer:

Phone Number:

Email:

Signer's Signature:

Thumb Print:

Service Performed:
- ○ Oath
- ○ Acknowledgment
- ○ Jurat
- ○ Other:

Identification:
- ○ I.D. Card
- ○ Drivers License
- ○ Passport
- ○ Other:
- ○ Credible Witness
- ○ Known Personally

I.D. Number:

Issued By:

Issued Date:

Expiration Date:

Document Type:

Date/Time Notarized: AM PM

Document Date:

Fee Charged:

Printed Name and Address of Witness:

Phone Number:

Email:

Witness' Signature:

Comments:

Record Number:
150

NOTARY RECORD

Printed Name and Address of Signer:	Phone Number:	Thumb Print:
	Email:	
	Signer's Signature:	

Service Performed:	Identification:	I.D. Number:	
O Oath	O I.D. Card O Credible Witness		
O Acknowledgment	O Drivers License O Known Personally	Issued By:	
O Jurat	O Passport	Issued Date:	Expiration Date:
O Other:	O Other:		
Document Type:	**Date/Time Notarized:** AM / PM	**Document Date:**	**Fee Charged:**

Printed Name and Address of Witness:	Phone Number:
	Email:
	Witness' Signature:

Comments:	Record Number:
	151

NOTARY RECORD

Printed Name and Address of Signer:	Phone Number:	Thumb Print:
	Email:	
	Signer's Signature:	

Service Performed:	Identification:	I.D. Number:	
O Oath	O I.D. Card O Credible Witness		
O Acknowledgment	O Drivers License O Known Personally	Issued By:	
O Jurat	O Passport	Issued Date:	Expiration Date:
O Other:	O Other:		
Document Type:	**Date/Time Notarized:** AM / PM	**Document Date:**	**Fee Charged:**

Printed Name and Address of Witness:	Phone Number:
	Email:
	Witness' Signature:

Comments:	Record Number:
	152

NOTARY RECORD

Printed Name and Address of Signer:

Phone Number:

Email:

Signer's Signature:

Thumb Print:

Service Performed:
- O Oath
- O Acknowledgment
- O Jurat
- O Other:

Identification:
- O I.D. Card
- O Drivers License
- O Passport
- O Other:
- O Credible Witness
- O Known Personally

I.D. Number:

Issued By:

Issued Date:

Expiration Date:

Document Type:

Date/Time Notarized: AM PM

Document Date:

Fee Charged:

Printed Name and Address of Witness:

Phone Number:

Email:

Witness' Signature:

Comments:

Record Number: 153

NOTARY RECORD

Printed Name and Address of Signer:

Phone Number:

Email:

Signer's Signature:

Thumb Print:

Service Performed:
- O Oath
- O Acknowledgment
- O Jurat
- O Other:

Identification:
- O I.D. Card
- O Drivers License
- O Passport
- O Other:
- O Credible Witness
- O Known Personally

I.D. Number:

Issued By:

Issued Date:

Expiration Date:

Document Type:

Date/Time Notarized: AM PM

Document Date:

Fee Charged:

Printed Name and Address of Witness:

Phone Number:

Email:

Witness' Signature:

Comments:

Record Number: 154

NOTARY RECORD

Printed Name and Address of Signer:	**Phone Number:**	**Thumb Print:**
	Email:	
	Signer's Signature:	

Service Performed:	**Identification:**		**I.D. Number:**	
O Oath	O I.D. Card	O Credible Witness		
O Acknowledgment	O Drivers License	O Known Personally	**Issued By:**	
O Jurat	O Passport		**Issued Date:**	**Expiration Date:**
O Other:	O Other:			
Document Type:	**Date/Time Notarized:**	AM PM	**Document Date:**	**Fee Charged:**

Printed Name and Address of Witness:	**Phone Number:**
	Email:
	Witness' Signature:

Comments:	**Record Number:**
	155

NOTARY RECORD

Printed Name and Address of Signer:	**Phone Number:**	**Thumb Print:**
	Email:	
	Signer's Signature:	

Service Performed:	**Identification:**		**I.D. Number:**	
O Oath	O I.D. Card	O Credible Witness		
O Acknowledgment	O Drivers License	O Known Personally	**Issued By:**	
O Jurat	O Passport		**Issued Date:**	**Expiration Date:**
O Other:	O Other:			
Document Type:	**Date/Time Notarized:**	AM PM	**Document Date:**	**Fee Charged:**

Printed Name and Address of Witness:	**Phone Number:**
	Email:
	Witness' Signature:

Comments:	**Record Number:**
	156

NOTARY RECORD

Printed Name and Address of Signer:	Phone Number:	Thumb Print:
	Email:	
	Signer's Signature:	

Service Performed:	Identification:	I.D. Number:	
○ Oath	○ I.D. Card ○ Credible Witness		
○ Acknowledgment	○ Drivers License ○ Known Personally	Issued By:	
○ Jurat	○ Passport	Issued Date:	Expiration Date:
○ Other:	○ Other:		
Document Type:	Date/Time Notarized: AM PM	Document Date:	Fee Charged:

Printed Name and Address of Witness:	Phone Number:
	Email:
	Witness' Signature:

Comments:	Record Number: **157**

NOTARY RECORD

Printed Name and Address of Signer:	Phone Number:	Thumb Print:
	Email:	
	Signer's Signature:	

Service Performed:	Identification:	I.D. Number:	
○ Oath	○ I.D. Card ○ Credible Witness		
○ Acknowledgment	○ Drivers License ○ Known Personally	Issued By:	
○ Jurat	○ Passport	Issued Date:	Expiration Date:
○ Other:	○ Other:		
Document Type:	Date/Time Notarized: AM PM	Document Date:	Fee Charged:

Printed Name and Address of Witness:	Phone Number:
	Email:
	Witness' Signature:

Comments:	Record Number: **158**

NOTARY RECORD

Printed Name and Address of Signer:	Phone Number:	Thumb Print:
	Email:	
	Signer's Signature:	

Service Performed:
- ○ Oath
- ○ Acknowledgment
- ○ Jurat
- ○ Other:

Identification:
- ○ I.D. Card   ○ Credible Witness
- ○ Drivers License   ○ Known Personally
- ○ Passport
- ○ Other:

I.D. Number:	
Issued By:	
Issued Date:	Expiration Date:

Document Type:	Date/Time Notarized: AM PM	Document Date:	Fee Charged:

Printed Name and Address of Witness:	Phone Number:
	Email:
	Witness' Signature:

Comments:

Record Number: 159

NOTARY RECORD

Printed Name and Address of Signer:	Phone Number:	Thumb Print:
	Email:	
	Signer's Signature:	

Service Performed:
- ○ Oath
- ○ Acknowledgment
- ○ Jurat
- ○ Other:

Identification:
- ○ I.D. Card   ○ Credible Witness
- ○ Drivers License   ○ Known Personally
- ○ Passport
- ○ Other:

I.D. Number:	
Issued By:	
Issued Date:	Expiration Date:

Document Type:	Date/Time Notarized: AM PM	Document Date:	Fee Charged:

Printed Name and Address of Witness:	Phone Number:
	Email:
	Witness' Signature:

Comments:

Record Number: 160

NOTARY RECORD

Printed Name and Address of Signer:	**Phone Number:**	**Thumb Print:**
	Email:	
	Signer's Signature:	

Service Performed:	**Identification:**	**I.D. Number:**	
○ Oath	○ I.D. Card ○ Credible Witness		
○ Acknowledgment	○ Drivers License ○ Known Personally	**Issued By:**	
○ Jurat	○ Passport		
○ Other:	○ Other:	**Issued Date:**	**Expiration Date:**
Document Type:	**Date/Time Notarized:** AM PM	**Document Date:**	**Fee Charged:**

Printed Name and Address of Witness:	**Phone Number:**
	Email:
	Witness' Signature:

Comments:	**Record Number:** **161**

NOTARY RECORD

Printed Name and Address of Signer:	**Phone Number:**	**Thumb Print:**
	Email:	
	Signer's Signature:	

Service Performed:	**Identification:**	**I.D. Number:**	
○ Oath	○ I.D. Card ○ Credible Witness		
○ Acknowledgment	○ Drivers License ○ Known Personally	**Issued By:**	
○ Jurat	○ Passport		
○ Other:	○ Other:	**Issued Date:**	**Expiration Date:**
Document Type:	**Date/Time Notarized:** AM PM	**Document Date:**	**Fee Charged:**

Printed Name and Address of Witness:	**Phone Number:**
	Email:
	Witness' Signature:

Comments:	**Record Number:** **162**

NOTARY RECORD

Printed Name and Address of Signer:	Phone Number:	Thumb Print:
	Email:	
	Signer's Signature:	

Service Performed:	Identification:	I.D. Number:	
O Oath	O I.D. Card O Credible Witness		
O Acknowledgment	O Drivers License O Known Personally	Issued By:	
O Jurat	O Passport		
O Other:	O Other:	Issued Date:	Expiration Date:
Document Type:	Date/Time Notarized: AM PM	Document Date:	Fee Charged:

Printed Name and Address of Witness:	Phone Number:
	Email:
	Witness' Signature:

Comments:	Record Number:
	163

NOTARY RECORD

Printed Name and Address of Signer:	Phone Number:	Thumb Print:
	Email:	
	Signer's Signature:	

Service Performed:	Identification:	I.D. Number:	
O Oath	O I.D. Card O Credible Witness		
O Acknowledgment	O Drivers License O Known Personally	Issued By:	
O Jurat	O Passport		
O Other:	O Other:	Issued Date:	Expiration Date:
Document Type:	Date/Time Notarized: AM PM	Document Date:	Fee Charged:

Printed Name and Address of Witness:	Phone Number:
	Email:
	Witness' Signature:

Comments:	Record Number:
	164

NOTARY RECORD

Printed Name and Address of Signer:	Phone Number:	Thumb Print:
	Email:	
	Signer's Signature:	

Service Performed:	Identification:	I.D. Number:
○ Oath	○ I.D. Card ○ Credible Witness	
○ Acknowledgment	○ Drivers License ○ Known Personally	Issued By:
○ Jurat	○ Passport	
○ Other:	○ Other:	Issued Date: Expiration Date:

Document Type:	Date/Time Notarized: AM / PM	Document Date:	Fee Charged:

Printed Name and Address of Witness:	Phone Number:
	Email:
	Witness' Signature:

Comments:

Record Number: 165

NOTARY RECORD

Printed Name and Address of Signer:	Phone Number:	Thumb Print:
	Email:	
	Signer's Signature:	

Service Performed:	Identification:	I.D. Number:
○ Oath	○ I.D. Card ○ Credible Witness	
○ Acknowledgment	○ Drivers License ○ Known Personally	Issued By:
○ Jurat	○ Passport	
○ Other:	○ Other:	Issued Date: Expiration Date:

Document Type:	Date/Time Notarized: AM / PM	Document Date:	Fee Charged:

Printed Name and Address of Witness:	Phone Number:
	Email:
	Witness' Signature:

Comments:

Record Number: 166

NOTARY RECORD

Printed Name and Address of Signer:	Phone Number:	Thumb Print:
	Email:	
	Signer's Signature:	

Service Performed:	Identification:	I.D. Number:
O Oath	O I.D. Card O Credible Witness	
O Acknowledgment	O Drivers License O Known Personally	Issued By:
O Jurat	O Passport	Issued Date: Expiration Date:
O Other:	O Other:	

Document Type:	Date/Time Notarized: AM / PM	Document Date:	Fee Charged:

Printed Name and Address of Witness:	Phone Number:
	Email:
	Witness' Signature:

Comments:	Record Number: **167**

NOTARY RECORD

Printed Name and Address of Signer:	Phone Number:	Thumb Print:
	Email:	
	Signer's Signature:	

Service Performed:	Identification:	I.D. Number:
O Oath	O I.D. Card O Credible Witness	
O Acknowledgment	O Drivers License O Known Personally	Issued By:
O Jurat	O Passport	Issued Date: Expiration Date:
O Other:	O Other:	

Document Type:	Date/Time Notarized: AM / PM	Document Date:	Fee Charged:

Printed Name and Address of Witness:	Phone Number:
	Email:
	Witness' Signature:

Comments:	Record Number: **168**

NOTARY RECORD

Printed Name and Address of Signer:

Phone Number:

Email:

Signer's Signature:

Thumb Print:

Service Performed:
- ○ Oath
- ○ Acknowledgment
- ○ Jurat
- ○ Other:

Identification:
- ○ I.D. Card
- ○ Drivers License
- ○ Passport
- ○ Other:
- ○ Credible Witness
- ○ Known Personally

I.D. Number:

Issued By:

Issued Date:

Expiration Date:

Document Type:

Date/Time Notarized: AM PM

Document Date:

Fee Charged:

Printed Name and Address of Witness:

Phone Number:

Email:

Witness' Signature:

Comments:

Record Number: 169

NOTARY RECORD

Printed Name and Address of Signer:

Phone Number:

Email:

Signer's Signature:

Thumb Print:

Service Performed:
- ○ Oath
- ○ Acknowledgment
- ○ Jurat
- ○ Other:

Identification:
- ○ I.D. Card
- ○ Drivers License
- ○ Passport
- ○ Other:
- ○ Credible Witness
- ○ Known Personally

I.D. Number:

Issued By:

Issued Date:

Expiration Date:

Document Type:

Date/Time Notarized: AM PM

Document Date:

Fee Charged:

Printed Name and Address of Witness:

Phone Number:

Email:

Witness' Signature:

Comments:

Record Number: 170

NOTARY RECORD

Printed Name and Address of Signer:

Phone Number:

Email:

Signer's Signature:

Thumb Print:

Service Performed:
- ○ Oath
- ○ Acknowledgment
- ○ Jurat
- ○ Other:

Identification:
- ○ I.D. Card
- ○ Drivers License
- ○ Passport
- ○ Other:
- ○ Credible Witness
- ○ Known Personally

I.D. Number:

Issued By:

Issued Date: | **Expiration Date:**

Document Type:

Date/Time Notarized: AM PM

Document Date: | **Fee Charged:**

Printed Name and Address of Witness:

Phone Number:

Email:

Witness' Signature:

Comments:

Record Number: 171

NOTARY RECORD

Printed Name and Address of Signer:

Phone Number:

Email:

Signer's Signature:

Thumb Print:

Service Performed:
- ○ Oath
- ○ Acknowledgment
- ○ Jurat
- ○ Other:

Identification:
- ○ I.D. Card
- ○ Drivers License
- ○ Passport
- ○ Other:
- ○ Credible Witness
- ○ Known Personally

I.D. Number:

Issued By:

Issued Date: | **Expiration Date:**

Document Type:

Date/Time Notarized: AM PM

Document Date: | **Fee Charged:**

Printed Name and Address of Witness:

Phone Number:

Email:

Witness' Signature:

Comments:

Record Number: 172

NOTARY RECORD

Printed Name and Address of Signer:

Phone Number:

Email:

Signer's Signature:

Thumb Print:

Service Performed:
- ○ Oath
- ○ Acknowledgment
- ○ Jurat
- ○ Other:

Identification:
- ○ I.D. Card
- ○ Drivers License
- ○ Passport
- ○ Other:
- ○ Credible Witness
- ○ Known Personally

I.D. Number:

Issued By:

Issued Date:

Expiration Date:

Document Type:

Date/Time Notarized: AM PM

Document Date:

Fee Charged:

Printed Name and Address of Witness:

Phone Number:

Email:

Witness' Signature:

Comments:

Record Number:
173

NOTARY RECORD

Printed Name and Address of Signer:

Phone Number:

Email:

Signer's Signature:

Thumb Print:

Service Performed:
- ○ Oath
- ○ Acknowledgment
- ○ Jurat
- ○ Other:

Identification:
- ○ I.D. Card
- ○ Drivers License
- ○ Passport
- ○ Other:
- ○ Credible Witness
- ○ Known Personally

I.D. Number:

Issued By:

Issued Date:

Expiration Date:

Document Type:

Date/Time Notarized: AM PM

Document Date:

Fee Charged:

Printed Name and Address of Witness:

Phone Number:

Email:

Witness' Signature:

Comments:

Record Number:
174

NOTARY RECORD

Printed Name and Address of Signer:	Phone Number:	Thumb Print:
	Email:	
	Signer's Signature:	

Service Performed:	Identification:	I.D. Number:	
○ Oath	○ I.D. Card ○ Credible Witness		
○ Acknowledgment	○ Drivers License ○ Known Personally	Issued By:	
○ Jurat	○ Passport	Issued Date:	Expiration Date:
○ Other:	○ Other:		
Document Type:	Date/Time Notarized: AM PM	Document Date:	Fee Charged:

Printed Name and Address of Witness:	Phone Number:
	Email:
	Witness' Signature:

Comments:	Record Number: **175**

NOTARY RECORD

Printed Name and Address of Signer:	Phone Number:	Thumb Print:
	Email:	
	Signer's Signature:	

Service Performed:	Identification:	I.D. Number:	
○ Oath	○ I.D. Card ○ Credible Witness		
○ Acknowledgment	○ Drivers License ○ Known Personally	Issued By:	
○ Jurat	○ Passport	Issued Date:	Expiration Date:
○ Other:	○ Other:		
Document Type:	Date/Time Notarized: AM PM	Document Date:	Fee Charged:

Printed Name and Address of Witness:	Phone Number:
	Email:
	Witness' Signature:

Comments:	Record Number: **176**

NOTARY RECORD

Printed Name and Address of Signer:

Phone Number:

Email:

Signer's Signature:

Thumb Print:

Service Performed:
- ○ Oath
- ○ Acknowledgment
- ○ Jurat
- ○ Other:

Identification:
- ○ I.D. Card
- ○ Drivers License
- ○ Passport
- ○ Other:
- ○ Credible Witness
- ○ Known Personally

I.D. Number:

Issued By:

Issued Date:

Expiration Date:

Document Type:

Date/Time Notarized: AM PM

Document Date:

Fee Charged:

Printed Name and Address of Witness:

Phone Number:

Email:

Witness' Signature:

Comments:

Record Number:
177

NOTARY RECORD

Printed Name and Address of Signer:

Phone Number:

Email:

Signer's Signature:

Thumb Print:

Service Performed:
- ○ Oath
- ○ Acknowledgment
- ○ Jurat
- ○ Other:

Identification:
- ○ I.D. Card
- ○ Drivers License
- ○ Passport
- ○ Other:
- ○ Credible Witness
- ○ Known Personally

I.D. Number:

Issued By:

Issued Date:

Expiration Date:

Document Type:

Date/Time Notarized: AM PM

Document Date:

Fee Charged:

Printed Name and Address of Witness:

Phone Number:

Email:

Witness' Signature:

Comments:

Record Number:
178

NOTARY RECORD

Printed Name and Address of Signer:	Phone Number:	Thumb Print:
	Email:	
	Signer's Signature:	

Service Performed:
- ○ Oath
- ○ Acknowledgment
- ○ Jurat
- ○ Other:

Identification:
- ○ I.D. Card   ○ Credible Witness
- ○ Drivers License   ○ Known Personally
- ○ Passport
- ○ Other:

I.D. Number:	
Issued By:	
Issued Date:	Expiration Date:

Document Type:	Date/Time Notarized: AM PM	Document Date:	Fee Charged:

Printed Name and Address of Witness:	Phone Number:
	Email:
	Witness' Signature:

Comments:	Record Number: **179**

NOTARY RECORD

Printed Name and Address of Signer:	Phone Number:	Thumb Print:
	Email:	
	Signer's Signature:	

Service Performed:
- ○ Oath
- ○ Acknowledgment
- ○ Jurat
- ○ Other:

Identification:
- ○ I.D. Card   ○ Credible Witness
- ○ Drivers License   ○ Known Personally
- ○ Passport
- ○ Other:

I.D. Number:	
Issued By:	
Issued Date:	Expiration Date:

Document Type:	Date/Time Notarized: AM PM	Document Date:	Fee Charged:

Printed Name and Address of Witness:	Phone Number:
	Email:
	Witness' Signature:

Comments:	Record Number: **180**

NOTARY RECORD

Printed Name and Address of Signer:

Phone Number:

Email:

Signer's Signature:

Thumb Print:

Service Performed:
- ○ Oath
- ○ Acknowledgment
- ○ Jurat
- ○ Other:

Identification:
- ○ I.D. Card
- ○ Drivers License
- ○ Passport
- ○ Other:
- ○ Credible Witness
- ○ Known Personally

I.D. Number:

Issued By:

Issued Date:

Expiration Date:

Document Type:

Date/Time Notarized: AM PM

Document Date:

Fee Charged:

Printed Name and Address of Witness:

Phone Number:

Email:

Witness' Signature:

Comments:

Record Number:
181

NOTARY RECORD

Printed Name and Address of Signer:

Phone Number:

Email:

Signer's Signature:

Thumb Print:

Service Performed:
- ○ Oath
- ○ Acknowledgment
- ○ Jurat
- ○ Other:

Identification:
- ○ I.D. Card
- ○ Drivers License
- ○ Passport
- ○ Other:
- ○ Credible Witness
- ○ Known Personally

I.D. Number:

Issued By:

Issued Date:

Expiration Date:

Document Type:

Date/Time Notarized: AM PM

Document Date:

Fee Charged:

Printed Name and Address of Witness:

Phone Number:

Email:

Witness' Signature:

Comments:

Record Number:
182

NOTARY RECORD

Printed Name and Address of Signer:

Phone Number:

Email:

Signer's Signature:

Thumb Print:

Service Performed:
- ○ Oath
- ○ Acknowledgment
- ○ Jurat
- ○ Other:

Identification:
- ○ I.D. Card
- ○ Drivers License
- ○ Passport
- ○ Other:
- ○ Credible Witness
- ○ Known Personally

I.D. Number:

Issued By:

Issued Date:

Expiration Date:

Document Type:

Date/Time Notarized: AM PM

Document Date:

Fee Charged:

Printed Name and Address of Witness:

Phone Number:

Email:

Witness' Signature:

Comments:

Record Number: 183

NOTARY RECORD

Printed Name and Address of Signer:

Phone Number:

Email:

Signer's Signature:

Thumb Print:

Service Performed:
- ○ Oath
- ○ Acknowledgment
- ○ Jurat
- ○ Other:

Identification:
- ○ I.D. Card
- ○ Drivers License
- ○ Passport
- ○ Other:
- ○ Credible Witness
- ○ Known Personally

I.D. Number:

Issued By:

Issued Date:

Expiration Date:

Document Type:

Date/Time Notarized: AM PM

Document Date:

Fee Charged:

Printed Name and Address of Witness:

Phone Number:

Email:

Witness' Signature:

Comments:

Record Number: 184

NOTARY RECORD

Printed Name and Address of Signer:

Phone Number:

Email:

Signer's Signature:

Thumb Print:

Service Performed:
- ○ Oath
- ○ Acknowledgment
- ○ Jurat
- ○ Other:

Identification:
- ○ I.D. Card
- ○ Drivers License
- ○ Passport
- ○ Other:
- ○ Credible Witness
- ○ Known Personally

I.D. Number:

Issued By:

Issued Date:

Expiration Date:

Document Type:

Date/Time Notarized: AM / PM

Document Date:

Fee Charged:

Printed Name and Address of Witness:

Phone Number:

Email:

Witness' Signature:

Comments:

Record Number: **185**

NOTARY RECORD

Printed Name and Address of Signer:

Phone Number:

Email:

Signer's Signature:

Thumb Print:

Service Performed:
- ○ Oath
- ○ Acknowledgment
- ○ Jurat
- ○ Other:

Identification:
- ○ I.D. Card
- ○ Drivers License
- ○ Passport
- ○ Other:
- ○ Credible Witness
- ○ Known Personally

I.D. Number:

Issued By:

Issued Date:

Expiration Date:

Document Type:

Date/Time Notarized: AM / PM

Document Date:

Fee Charged:

Printed Name and Address of Witness:

Phone Number:

Email:

Witness' Signature:

Comments:

Record Number: **186**

NOTARY RECORD

Printed Name and Address of Signer:	Phone Number:	Thumb Print:
	Email:	
	Signer's Signature:	

Service Performed:
- O Oath
- O Acknowledgment
- O Jurat
- O Other:

Identification:
- O I.D. Card   O Credible Witness
- O Drivers License   O Known Personally
- O Passport
- O Other:

I.D. Number:	
Issued By:	
Issued Date:	Expiration Date:

Document Type:	Date/Time Notarized: AM PM	Document Date:	Fee Charged:

Printed Name and Address of Witness:	Phone Number:
	Email:
	Witness' Signature:

Comments:	Record Number: **187**

NOTARY RECORD

Printed Name and Address of Signer:	Phone Number:	Thumb Print:
	Email:	
	Signer's Signature:	

Service Performed:
- O Oath
- O Acknowledgment
- O Jurat
- O Other:

Identification:
- O I.D. Card   O Credible Witness
- O Drivers License   O Known Personally
- O Passport
- O Other:

I.D. Number:	
Issued By:	
Issued Date:	Expiration Date:

Document Type:	Date/Time Notarized: AM PM	Document Date:	Fee Charged:

Printed Name and Address of Witness:	Phone Number:
	Email:
	Witness' Signature:

Comments:	Record Number: **188**

NOTARY RECORD

Printed Name and Address of Signer:

Phone Number:

Email:

Signer's Signature:

Thumb Print:

Service Performed:
- ○ Oath
- ○ Acknowledgment
- ○ Jurat
- ○ Other:

Identification:
- ○ I.D. Card
- ○ Drivers License
- ○ Passport
- ○ Other:
- ○ Credible Witness
- ○ Known Personally

I.D. Number:

Issued By:

Issued Date:

Expiration Date:

Document Type:

Date/Time Notarized: AM PM

Document Date:

Fee Charged:

Printed Name and Address of Witness:

Phone Number:

Email:

Witness' Signature:

Comments:

Record Number:
189

NOTARY RECORD

Printed Name and Address of Signer:

Phone Number:

Email:

Signer's Signature:

Thumb Print:

Service Performed:
- ○ Oath
- ○ Acknowledgment
- ○ Jurat
- ○ Other:

Identification:
- ○ I.D. Card
- ○ Drivers License
- ○ Passport
- ○ Other:
- ○ Credible Witness
- ○ Known Personally

I.D. Number:

Issued By:

Issued Date:

Expiration Date:

Document Type:

Date/Time Notarized: AM PM

Document Date:

Fee Charged:

Printed Name and Address of Witness:

Phone Number:

Email:

Witness' Signature:

Comments:

Record Number:
190

NOTARY RECORD

Printed Name and Address of Signer:

Phone Number:

Email:

Signer's Signature:

Thumb Print:

Service Performed:
- Oath
- Acknowledgment
- Jurat
- Other:

Identification:
- I.D. Card
- Drivers License
- Passport
- Other:
- Credible Witness
- Known Personally

I.D. Number:

Issued By:

Issued Date:

Expiration Date:

Document Type:

Date/Time Notarized: AM PM

Document Date:

Fee Charged:

Printed Name and Address of Witness:

Phone Number:

Email:

Witness' Signature:

Comments:

Record Number: 191

NOTARY RECORD

Printed Name and Address of Signer:

Phone Number:

Email:

Signer's Signature:

Thumb Print:

Service Performed:
- Oath
- Acknowledgment
- Jurat
- Other:

Identification:
- I.D. Card
- Drivers License
- Passport
- Other:
- Credible Witness
- Known Personally

I.D. Number:

Issued By:

Issued Date:

Expiration Date:

Document Type:

Date/Time Notarized: AM PM

Document Date:

Fee Charged:

Printed Name and Address of Witness:

Phone Number:

Email:

Witness' Signature:

Comments:

Record Number: 192

NOTARY RECORD

Printed Name and Address of Signer:	Phone Number:	Thumb Print:
	Email:	
	Signer's Signature:	

Service Performed:	Identification:	I.D. Number:
O Oath	O I.D. Card O Credible Witness	
O Acknowledgment	O Drivers License O Known Personally	Issued By:
O Jurat	O Passport	Issued Date: Expiration Date:
O Other:	O Other:	
Document Type:	**Date/Time Notarized:** AM PM	**Document Date:** **Fee Charged:**

Printed Name and Address of Witness:	Phone Number:
	Email:
	Witness' Signature:

Comments:	Record Number: **193**

NOTARY RECORD

Printed Name and Address of Signer:	Phone Number:	Thumb Print:
	Email:	
	Signer's Signature:	

Service Performed:	Identification:	I.D. Number:
O Oath	O I.D. Card O Credible Witness	
O Acknowledgment	O Drivers License O Known Personally	Issued By:
O Jurat	O Passport	Issued Date: Expiration Date:
O Other:	O Other:	
Document Type:	**Date/Time Notarized:** AM PM	**Document Date:** **Fee Charged:**

Printed Name and Address of Witness:	Phone Number:
	Email:
	Witness' Signature:

Comments:	Record Number: **194**

NOTARY RECORD

Printed Name and Address of Signer:

Phone Number:

Email:

Signer's Signature:

Thumb Print:

Service Performed:
- ○ Oath
- ○ Acknowledgment
- ○ Jurat
- ○ Other:

Identification:
- ○ I.D. Card
- ○ Drivers License
- ○ Passport
- ○ Other:
- ○ Credible Witness
- ○ Known Personally

I.D. Number:

Issued By:

Issued Date:

Expiration Date:

Document Type:

Date/Time Notarized: AM PM

Document Date:

Fee Charged:

Printed Name and Address of Witness:

Phone Number:

Email:

Witness' Signature:

Comments:

Record Number: 195

NOTARY RECORD

Printed Name and Address of Signer:

Phone Number:

Email:

Signer's Signature:

Thumb Print:

Service Performed:
- ○ Oath
- ○ Acknowledgment
- ○ Jurat
- ○ Other:

Identification:
- ○ I.D. Card
- ○ Drivers License
- ○ Passport
- ○ Other:
- ○ Credible Witness
- ○ Known Personally

I.D. Number:

Issued By:

Issued Date:

Expiration Date:

Document Type:

Date/Time Notarized: AM PM

Document Date:

Fee Charged:

Printed Name and Address of Witness:

Phone Number:

Email:

Witness' Signature:

Comments:

Record Number: 196

NOTARY RECORD

Printed Name and Address of Signer:

Phone Number:

Email:

Signer's Signature:

Thumb Print:

Service Performed:
- ◯ Oath
- ◯ Acknowledgment
- ◯ Jurat
- ◯ Other:

Identification:
- ◯ I.D. Card   ◯ Credible Witness
- ◯ Drivers License   ◯ Known Personally
- ◯ Passport
- ◯ Other:

I.D. Number:

Issued By:

Issued Date: **Expiration Date:**

Document Type: **Date/Time Notarized:**   AM / PM   **Document Date:**   **Fee Charged:**

Printed Name and Address of Witness:

Phone Number:

Email:

Witness' Signature:

Comments:

Record Number: 197

NOTARY RECORD

Printed Name and Address of Signer:

Phone Number:

Email:

Signer's Signature:

Thumb Print:

Service Performed:
- ◯ Oath
- ◯ Acknowledgment
- ◯ Jurat
- ◯ Other:

Identification:
- ◯ I.D. Card   ◯ Credible Witness
- ◯ Drivers License   ◯ Known Personally
- ◯ Passport
- ◯ Other:

I.D. Number:

Issued By:

Issued Date: **Expiration Date:**

Document Type: **Date/Time Notarized:**   AM / PM   **Document Date:**   **Fee Charged:**

Printed Name and Address of Witness:

Phone Number:

Email:

Witness' Signature:

Comments:

Record Number: 198

NOTARY RECORD

Printed Name and Address of Signer:	Phone Number:	Thumb Print:
	Email:	
	Signer's Signature:	

Service Performed:
- ◯ Oath
- ◯ Acknowledgment
- ◯ Jurat
- ◯ Other:

Identification:
- ◯ I.D. Card   ◯ Credible Witness
- ◯ Drivers License   ◯ Known Personally
- ◯ Passport
- ◯ Other:

I.D. Number:	
Issued By:	
Issued Date:	Expiration Date:

Document Type:	Date/Time Notarized: AM PM	Document Date:	Fee Charged:

Printed Name and Address of Witness:	Phone Number:
	Email:
	Witness' Signature:

Comments:	Record Number: **199**

NOTARY RECORD

Printed Name and Address of Signer:	Phone Number:	Thumb Print:
	Email:	
	Signer's Signature:	

Service Performed:
- ◯ Oath
- ◯ Acknowledgment
- ◯ Jurat
- ◯ Other:

Identification:
- ◯ I.D. Card   ◯ Credible Witness
- ◯ Drivers License   ◯ Known Personally
- ◯ Passport
- ◯ Other:

I.D. Number:	
Issued By:	
Issued Date:	Expiration Date:

Document Type:	Date/Time Notarized: AM PM	Document Date:	Fee Charged:

Printed Name and Address of Witness:	Phone Number:
	Email:
	Witness' Signature:

Comments:	Record Number: **200**

NOTARY RECORD

Printed Name and Address of Signer:

Phone Number:

Email:

Signer's Signature:

Thumb Print:

Service Performed:
- ○ Oath
- ○ Acknowledgment
- ○ Jurat
- ○ Other:

Identification:
- ○ I.D. Card
- ○ Drivers License
- ○ Passport
- ○ Other:
- ○ Credible Witness
- ○ Known Personally

I.D. Number:

Issued By:

Issued Date:

Expiration Date:

Document Type:

Date/Time Notarized: AM PM

Document Date:

Fee Charged:

Printed Name and Address of Witness:

Phone Number:

Email:

Witness' Signature:

Comments:

Record Number: 201

NOTARY RECORD

Printed Name and Address of Signer:

Phone Number:

Email:

Signer's Signature:

Thumb Print:

Service Performed:
- ○ Oath
- ○ Acknowledgment
- ○ Jurat
- ○ Other:

Identification:
- ○ I.D. Card
- ○ Drivers License
- ○ Passport
- ○ Other:
- ○ Credible Witness
- ○ Known Personally

I.D. Number:

Issued By:

Issued Date:

Expiration Date:

Document Type:

Date/Time Notarized: AM PM

Document Date:

Fee Charged:

Printed Name and Address of Witness:

Phone Number:

Email:

Witness' Signature:

Comments:

Record Number: 202

NOTARY RECORD

Printed Name and Address of Signer:

Phone Number:

Email:

Signer's Signature:

Thumb Print:

Service Performed:
- ○ Oath
- ○ Acknowledgment
- ○ Jurat
- ○ Other:

Identification:
- ○ I.D. Card
- ○ Drivers License
- ○ Passport
- ○ Other:
- ○ Credible Witness
- ○ Known Personally

I.D. Number:

Issued By:

Issued Date:

Expiration Date:

Document Type:

Date/Time Notarized: AM / PM

Document Date:

Fee Charged:

Printed Name and Address of Witness:

Phone Number:

Email:

Witness' Signature:

Comments:

Record Number: 203

NOTARY RECORD

Printed Name and Address of Signer:

Phone Number:

Email:

Signer's Signature:

Thumb Print:

Service Performed:
- ○ Oath
- ○ Acknowledgment
- ○ Jurat
- ○ Other:

Identification:
- ○ I.D. Card
- ○ Drivers License
- ○ Passport
- ○ Other:
- ○ Credible Witness
- ○ Known Personally

I.D. Number:

Issued By:

Issued Date:

Expiration Date:

Document Type:

Date/Time Notarized: AM / PM

Document Date:

Fee Charged:

Printed Name and Address of Witness:

Phone Number:

Email:

Witness' Signature:

Comments:

Record Number: 204

NOTARY RECORD

Printed Name and Address of Signer:

Phone Number:

Email:

Signer's Signature:

Thumb Print:

Service Performed:
- ○ Oath
- ○ Acknowledgment
- ○ Jurat
- ○ Other:

Identification:
- ○ I.D. Card
- ○ Drivers License
- ○ Passport
- ○ Other:
- ○ Credible Witness
- ○ Known Personally

I.D. Number:

Issued By:

Issued Date:

Expiration Date:

Document Type:

Date/Time Notarized: AM / PM

Document Date:

Fee Charged:

Printed Name and Address of Witness:

Phone Number:

Email:

Witness' Signature:

Comments:

Record Number: 205

NOTARY RECORD

Printed Name and Address of Signer:

Phone Number:

Email:

Signer's Signature:

Thumb Print:

Service Performed:
- ○ Oath
- ○ Acknowledgment
- ○ Jurat
- ○ Other:

Identification:
- ○ I.D. Card
- ○ Drivers License
- ○ Passport
- ○ Other:
- ○ Credible Witness
- ○ Known Personally

I.D. Number:

Issued By:

Issued Date:

Expiration Date:

Document Type:

Date/Time Notarized: AM / PM

Document Date:

Fee Charged:

Printed Name and Address of Witness:

Phone Number:

Email:

Witness' Signature:

Comments:

Record Number: 206

NOTARY RECORD

Printed Name and Address of Signer:	Phone Number:	Thumb Print:
	Email:	
	Signer's Signature:	

Service Performed:
- ○ Oath
- ○ Acknowledgment
- ○ Jurat
- ○ Other:

Identification:
- ○ I.D. Card   ○ Credible Witness
- ○ Drivers License   ○ Known Personally
- ○ Passport
- ○ Other:

I.D. Number:

Issued By:

Issued Date:	Expiration Date:

Document Type:	Date/Time Notarized: AM PM	Document Date:	Fee Charged:

Printed Name and Address of Witness:	Phone Number:
	Email:
	Witness' Signature:

Comments:

Record Number: 207

NOTARY RECORD

Printed Name and Address of Signer:	Phone Number:	Thumb Print:
	Email:	
	Signer's Signature:	

Service Performed:
- ○ Oath
- ○ Acknowledgment
- ○ Jurat
- ○ Other:

Identification:
- ○ I.D. Card   ○ Credible Witness
- ○ Drivers License   ○ Known Personally
- ○ Passport
- ○ Other:

I.D. Number:

Issued By:

Issued Date:	Expiration Date:

Document Type:	Date/Time Notarized: AM PM	Document Date:	Fee Charged:

Printed Name and Address of Witness:	Phone Number:
	Email:
	Witness' Signature:

Comments:

Record Number: 208

NOTARY RECORD

Printed Name and Address of Signer:	Phone Number:	Thumb Print:
	Email:	
	Signer's Signature:	

Service Performed:	Identification:	I.D. Number:
○ Oath	○ I.D. Card ○ Credible Witness	
○ Acknowledgment	○ Drivers License ○ Known Personally	Issued By:
○ Jurat	○ Passport	Issued Date: Expiration Date:
○ Other:	○ Other:	

Document Type:	Date/Time Notarized: AM / PM	Document Date:	Fee Charged:

Printed Name and Address of Witness:	Phone Number:
	Email:
	Witness' Signature:

Comments:	Record Number: **209**

NOTARY RECORD

Printed Name and Address of Signer:	Phone Number:	Thumb Print:
	Email:	
	Signer's Signature:	

Service Performed:	Identification:	I.D. Number:
○ Oath	○ I.D. Card ○ Credible Witness	
○ Acknowledgment	○ Drivers License ○ Known Personally	Issued By:
○ Jurat	○ Passport	Issued Date: Expiration Date:
○ Other:	○ Other:	

Document Type:	Date/Time Notarized: AM / PM	Document Date:	Fee Charged:

Printed Name and Address of Witness:	Phone Number:
	Email:
	Witness' Signature:

Comments:	Record Number: **210**

NOTARY RECORD

Printed Name and Address of Signer:	Phone Number:	Thumb Print:
	Email:	
	Signer's Signature:	

Service Performed:
- ○ Oath
- ○ Acknowledgment
- ○ Jurat
- ○ Other:

Identification:
- ○ I.D. Card   ○ Credible Witness
- ○ Drivers License   ○ Known Personally
- ○ Passport
- ○ Other:

I.D. Number:	
Issued By:	
Issued Date:	Expiration Date:

Document Type:	Date/Time Notarized: AM / PM	Document Date:	Fee Charged:

Printed Name and Address of Witness:	Phone Number:
	Email:
	Witness' Signature:

Comments:

Record Number: 211

NOTARY RECORD

Printed Name and Address of Signer:	Phone Number:	Thumb Print:
	Email:	
	Signer's Signature:	

Service Performed:
- ○ Oath
- ○ Acknowledgment
- ○ Jurat
- ○ Other:

Identification:
- ○ I.D. Card   ○ Credible Witness
- ○ Drivers License   ○ Known Personally
- ○ Passport
- ○ Other:

I.D. Number:	
Issued By:	
Issued Date:	Expiration Date:

Document Type:	Date/Time Notarized: AM / PM	Document Date:	Fee Charged:

Printed Name and Address of Witness:	Phone Number:
	Email:
	Witness' Signature:

Comments:

Record Number: 212

NOTARY RECORD

Printed Name and Address of Signer:

Phone Number:

Email:

Signer's Signature:

Thumb Print:

Service Performed:
- ○ Oath
- ○ Acknowledgment
- ○ Jurat
- ○ Other:

Identification:
- ○ I.D. Card   ○ Credible Witness
- ○ Drivers License   ○ Known Personally
- ○ Passport
- ○ Other:

I.D. Number:

Issued By:

Issued Date:

Expiration Date:

Document Type:

Date/Time Notarized: AM PM

Document Date:

Fee Charged:

Printed Name and Address of Witness:

Phone Number:

Email:

Witness' Signature:

Comments:

Record Number:
213

NOTARY RECORD

Printed Name and Address of Signer:

Phone Number:

Email:

Signer's Signature:

Thumb Print:

Service Performed:
- ○ Oath
- ○ Acknowledgment
- ○ Jurat
- ○ Other:

Identification:
- ○ I.D. Card   ○ Credible Witness
- ○ Drivers License   ○ Known Personally
- ○ Passport
- ○ Other:

I.D. Number:

Issued By:

Issued Date:

Expiration Date:

Document Type:

Date/Time Notarized: AM PM

Document Date:

Fee Charged:

Printed Name and Address of Witness:

Phone Number:

Email:

Witness' Signature:

Comments:

Record Number:
214

NOTARY RECORD

Printed Name and Address of Signer:	Phone Number:	Thumb Print:
	Email:	
	Signer's Signature:	

Service Performed:	Identification:	I.D. Number:
O Oath	O I.D. Card O Credible Witness	
O Acknowledgment	O Drivers License O Known Personally	Issued By:
O Jurat	O Passport	
O Other:	O Other:	Issued Date: Expiration Date:
Document Type:	Date/Time Notarized: AM PM	Document Date: Fee Charged:

Printed Name and Address of Witness:	Phone Number:
	Email:
	Witness' Signature:

Comments:	Record Number: **215**

NOTARY RECORD

Printed Name and Address of Signer:	Phone Number:	Thumb Print:
	Email:	
	Signer's Signature:	

Service Performed:	Identification:	I.D. Number:
O Oath	O I.D. Card O Credible Witness	
O Acknowledgment	O Drivers License O Known Personally	Issued By:
O Jurat	O Passport	
O Other:	O Other:	Issued Date: Expiration Date:
Document Type:	Date/Time Notarized: AM PM	Document Date: Fee Charged:

Printed Name and Address of Witness:	Phone Number:
	Email:
	Witness' Signature:

Comments:	Record Number: **216**

NOTARY RECORD

Printed Name and Address of Signer:

Phone Number:

Email:

Signer's Signature:

Thumb Print:

Service Performed:
- ○ Oath
- ○ Acknowledgment
- ○ Jurat
- ○ Other:

Identification:
- ○ I.D. Card
- ○ Drivers License
- ○ Passport
- ○ Other:
- ○ Credible Witness
- ○ Known Personally

I.D. Number:

Issued By:

Issued Date:

Expiration Date:

Document Type:

Date/Time Notarized: AM PM

Document Date:

Fee Charged:

Printed Name and Address of Witness:

Phone Number:

Email:

Witness' Signature:

Comments:

Record Number: 217

NOTARY RECORD

Printed Name and Address of Signer:

Phone Number:

Email:

Signer's Signature:

Thumb Print:

Service Performed:
- ○ Oath
- ○ Acknowledgment
- ○ Jurat
- ○ Other:

Identification:
- ○ I.D. Card
- ○ Drivers License
- ○ Passport
- ○ Other:
- ○ Credible Witness
- ○ Known Personally

I.D. Number:

Issued By:

Issued Date:

Expiration Date:

Document Type:

Date/Time Notarized: AM PM

Document Date:

Fee Charged:

Printed Name and Address of Witness:

Phone Number:

Email:

Witness' Signature:

Comments:

Record Number: 218

NOTARY RECORD

Printed Name and Address of Signer:

Phone Number:

Email:

Signer's Signature:

Thumb Print:

Service Performed:
- ○ Oath
- ○ Acknowledgment
- ○ Jurat
- ○ Other:

Identification:
- ○ I.D. Card
- ○ Drivers License
- ○ Passport
- ○ Other:
- ○ Credible Witness
- ○ Known Personally

I.D. Number:

Issued By:

Issued Date:

Expiration Date:

Document Type:

Date/Time Notarized: AM / PM

Document Date:

Fee Charged:

Printed Name and Address of Witness:

Phone Number:

Email:

Witness' Signature:

Comments:

Record Number: 219

NOTARY RECORD

Printed Name and Address of Signer:

Phone Number:

Email:

Signer's Signature:

Thumb Print:

Service Performed:
- ○ Oath
- ○ Acknowledgment
- ○ Jurat
- ○ Other:

Identification:
- ○ I.D. Card
- ○ Drivers License
- ○ Passport
- ○ Other:
- ○ Credible Witness
- ○ Known Personally

I.D. Number:

Issued By:

Issued Date:

Expiration Date:

Document Type:

Date/Time Notarized: AM / PM

Document Date:

Fee Charged:

Printed Name and Address of Witness:

Phone Number:

Email:

Witness' Signature:

Comments:

Record Number: 220

Made in the USA
Las Vegas, NV
23 July 2024